Through Her Eyes

Bible Studies on Women in Scripture

Deborah Spink Winters, editor

JUDSON PRESS
PUBLISHERS SINCE 1824
VALLEY FORGE, PA

Through Her Eyes: Bible Studies on Women in Scripture

Judson Press has made every effort to trace the ownership of all quotes. In the event of a question arising from the use of a quote, we regret any error made and will be pleased to make the necessary correction in future printings and editions of this book.

Unless otherwise noted, Bible quotations in this volume are from New Revised Standard Version, copyright 1989, Division of Christian Education of the National Council of the Churches of Christ in the United States of America. Used by permission. All rights reserved.

Scripture quotations marked CEB are from the Common English Bible, copyright © 2011 Common English Bible. Used by permission. All rights reserved.

Scripture quotations marked KJV are from the King James Version of the Bible.

Scripture quotations marked MSG are from *THE MESSAGE.* Copyright © by Eugene H. Peterson 1993, 1994, 1995, 1996, 2000, 2001, 2002. Used by permission of NavPress Publishing Group.

Scripture quotations marked RSV are from the Revised Standard Version of the Bible, copyright 1952 [2nd edition, 1971] by the Division of Christian Education of the National Council of the Churches of Christ in the United States. Used by permission. All rights reserved.

Interior design by Crystal Devine.
Cover design by Wendy Ronga, Hampton Design Group.

Library of Congress Cataloging-in-Publication Data

Through her eyes : Bible studies on women in scripture / Deborah Winters, editor. -- first [edition].
    pages cm
  ISBN 978-0-8170-1769-9 (pbk. : alk. paper) 1. Women in the Bible--Biography.
I. Winters, Deborah, editor.
  BS575.T535 2016
  220.9'2082--dc23
                        2015022226

Printed in the U.S.A.

First printing, 2016.

Contents

Introduction

In January 2014 I began to teach one of my favorite courses at Palmer Theological Seminary, BIBL 632: Women in the Bible. I met nineteen seminary students eager to learn about the women in the Bible and what impact these ancient women's stories could have on their lives and ministries. I teach this class as a seminar where the students are expected to come to class fully prepared to discuss and interact with the material. To create a safe place so that deep sharing could occur, during our first class we created and agreed to the following behavioral covenant:

BIBL 632 Women in the Bible
Class Covenant

Confidentiality:
> What goes on in the classroom stays in the classroom except if someone is going to do harm to themselves or someone else.
> You can share biblical material but not personal material that was shared in the class with someone outside of the class.
> Use wisdom in what you share.

Taping:
> It is okay to tape lecture material, BUT if someone is sharing personal material, stop the tape.

Respect:
> Speak in "I statements" and don't generalize (i.e., "all" does not apply).

This is a "No Judgment Zone," meaning you are to respect where someone else is coming from even if you
don't agree.

Try not to "fix" someone unless you are asked.

Try not to take things personally.

Each person will take responsibility if the discussion goes
too far to tell the class we need a "time out."

Do not interrupt!

We invited God to be a part of our class and agreed to
start each class with a devotion led by one of the students.
We began by learning about the context of various women in
the Bible, starting with Eve (and Lilith), and then Sarah and
Hagar. As the class progressed, not only did these ancient
women begin to touch our lives in a very personal way, but
God showed up as well!

Students developed a strong desire to recreate this experience and study the women of the Bible in their own diverse
ministry settings. I challenged them with the idea of writing a
book so that others, whether individually or as a small group
or Bible study group, could also learn what lessons these ancient biblical women offer. A consensus was reached after a
class discussion and individual and collective prayer. Rather
than a traditional final presentation in the class, each student
would develop a chapter for the book as a culminating proj-
ect. We agreed on three goals for each of our chapters:

1. helping the reader contrast and compare how women
   in the Bible help inform healthier relationships today,
2. empowering the reader to think critically about the biblical text, and
3. giving the reader permission to ask difficult questions
   of the biblical text to challenge paradigms of women in
   today's society.

Thus this book was born in a seminary class.

How to Use This Book

This book can be used as either a personal devotional book or as a small group or Bible study book. The book is set up as follows:

Epigraph. A brief quote is provided at the beginning of each chapter to focus readers on an aspect of the biblical woman's character.

Hook Question. A question is posed for self-reflection on how readers would respond to a given situation based on the life of the biblical woman.

Biblical Story. The heart of the biblical story about the woman being studied is provided from the New Revised Standard Version, along with other possible biblical references for further study.

Biblical Exposition. A short explanation of the biblical setting of the story is given.

Personal Story. The author of the chapter reflects on how the woman's story in the Bible has touched her or his life.

Questions. Questions are posed for readers to discuss, reflect on, or journal or blog about how the biblical woman's story and the author's personal story have touched their lives.

Thought for Your Day. A sentence or phrase is used to focus on a point the material teaches.

Closing Prayer. A written prayer is provided. Readers are encouraged to pray beyond the written prayer, trusting the Holy Spirit to guide their thoughts and words as the material touches their lives.

About the Writer. A short autobiography of each chapter's author is given so that readers can have a better understanding of each chapter's personal story.

As a Small Group or Bible Study Resource

When using this book as a small group or Bible study resource, you have the option of accessing the extra material given online for small group leaders at www.judsonpress. com/free_download_book_excerpts.cfm.

Read through the small group leader's material, paying particular attention to the goals and teaching points for each chapter. Read through the entire chapter before presenting it to your small group. Ask the Holy Spirit to guide your preparation and to bless each person who will be studying with you.

This material is put together in such a way that it can be read during your small group or Bible study experience. If possible, however, ask each member of your group to work through the chapter and each of the questions before coming to your group meeting. This will allow plenty of time for all members to share their answers to the questions and to tell how the material has touched their lives.

I strongly suggest three things for the group leader:

1. Pray before your small group meeting, asking God to guide the discussion that needs to happen between your members, and trust that the Holy Spirit will show up.
2. At your very first session, create your own group behavioral covenant to help make your meeting a safe place for each of your members to share at a deep level.
3. Be willing to take the first step by telling how each chapter has affected you, and share a personal story from your own life if God leads you to do so.

Start each meeting by having each member of the group, including yourself, answer the Hook Question. Read the biblical text and the personal story aloud (unless participants have read it at home) or share a personal story from your life that relates to the biblical text. Give each person an opportunity to answer the questions at the end of the chapter and use the additional questions found in the leader's online resource. Always end your meeting by reading aloud as a group the written closing prayer, or use a devotional prepared by you or one of your members based on the chapter's material.

I'm confident that as you work your way through this book, God will show up in your life and in the lives of your small-group members. If you have any suggestions on how to make this material more beneficial to you or your ministry setting, please let me know via email at dwinters@eastern.edu!

God bless,
Rev. Dr. Deborah Spink Winters

Part 1

Women Who Were Healed

1

Woman with the Issue of Blood
Coming Out of the Dark

CLESHA STATEN

> *Owning our story and loving ourselves through that*
> *process is the bravest thing that we will ever do.*
> —BRENÉ BROWN, *THE GIFTS OF IMPERFECTION*

Hook Question

How long will you hemorrhage?

Biblical Story

MARK 5:25-34

Now there was a woman who had been suffering from hemorrhages for twelve years. She had endured much under many physicians, and had spent all that she had; and she was no better, but rather grew worse. She had heard about Jesus, and came up behind him in the crowd and touched his cloak, for she said, "If I but touch his clothes, I will be made well." Immediately her hemorrhage stopped; and she felt in her body that she was healed of her disease. Immediately aware that power had gone forth from him, Jesus turned about in the crowd and said, "Who touched my clothes?" And his disciples said to him, "You see the crowd pressing in on you; how can you say, 'Who touched me?'" He looked all around to see who had done it. But the woman, knowing what had happened to her, came in fear and trembling, fell down before him, and told him the whole truth. He said to her, "Daughter, your faith has made you well; go in peace, and be healed of your disease."

Biblical Exposition

When someone reads this story, the first thing that may come to mind is that this woman is physically hemorrhaging. And some biblical scholars will agree, the hemorrhaging is most likely related to a "womanly issue." Yes, *that* womanly issue. As was the custom, women of that day were separated from the community because menstrual (or postpartum) bleeding made them ritually unclean. I can only imagine the despair this woman felt as she lived alone for twelve years with nothing more than a tent and a mat. Those around her saw her as unclean, but that wasn't where her story ended.

Somehow, she heard about Jesus and knew he was one option to receive healing. Touching his cloak brought her physical healing, but I can't help thinking that, emotionally and spiritually, she was still hemorrhaging. After so many years, would those around her have persisted in avoiding her, shunning her for her "contagious" past? And even after showing herself to the priests, making the necessary sacrifices, and being declared ritually clean again, would she continue to bear the stigma and shame of her past—in her own mind as well as in the minds of her neighbors?

This woman had lived in isolation from her community, in a continuous state of ritual uncleanness, for more than a decade—probably her entire adult life. She had lived her life in the shadows of her former self, being careful not to come in contact with anyone as she moved about, seeking help from those who were not equipped to help her. Was physical healing sufficient to arrest the spiritual and psychological hemorrhaging deep inside? How would she discover the wholeness that would allow her to live into her new identity as a woman transformed by the healing power of Jesus?

Personal Story

When I read this story, it causes me to reflect on my own years of hemorrhaging. Unlike this woman's physical bleeding, my hemorrhaging was emotional and spiritual. As a survivor of rape, I carried the feelings of guilt and shame as well as the feeling that I was unclean and unworthy. Even in a roomful of people, I felt alone and isolated—emotionally cut off from everyone. I was living alone in a "tent," wearing a mask to protect what little piece of myself I was able to retain.

Emotionally I was in search of something I would never be able to obtain from any person, place, or thing. I sought help, but I didn't find healing. It took years for me to recognize that I was hemorrhaging and even more time to recognize that my healing was in Jesus. Intellectually, as a Christian woman, I knew this to be true. I knew that Jesus heals and my hope and salvation begin and end with him. I knew this, but how I felt was completely different.

I believed Jesus' healing was available for everyone—except me. I was spiritually hemorrhaging. It was as if I was leaving a spiritual blood trail of myself wherever I went. I was still in that dark tent hiding from everyone, including Christ. It is in this place of darkness where my story intersects with this woman from so many years ago. We were both standing on the edge of complete healing if only we were willing to step out and tell him "the whole truth." Our whole truth— the good, the bad, and the downright ugly.

In this one act of stepping out into the light, we can escape the dark. When we give voice to our pain, we can receive the healing we seek. When we are willing to confess everything before the Lord, we can be reconciled with those we love, including ourselves. Jesus already knows my story, but my verbalizing it generates power.

When I lived in the tent, loneliness and a sense of unworthiness kept me company. I had to make the decision to step out of the dark and leave behind the notion that I was unworthy of love, happiness, and peace. I had to embrace the truth, and the truth is that Jesus is bigger than my pain. Jesus is my way back to my God, my community, and myself. His healing is the only way I could be *completely* healed, the only way my hemorrhaging could be stopped. I had to be willing to step out of my darkness and tell my whole truth.

Questions

1. What are you holding on to that is causing you to hemorrhage, whether emotionally, spiritually, mentally, or physically?
2. When in your life have you felt unclean or unworthy of healing or redemption?
3. Jesus was on his way to heal someone else when this woman reached out to touch him (see Mark 5:21-24). How would you feel if you were the woman and knew that you had interrupted the healing of someone else?
4. What keeps you from stepping forward to tell your whole story to Jesus? What empowers you to speak the whole truth about your darkness?

Thought for Your Day

No matter where you may be in your life, Jesus can call you out of the darkness and into his restoring light.

Closing Prayer

God, we thank you. We thank you that even in the moments when we are hemorrhaging we can reach out to you and be healed. Lord, help me to step out of the darkness and into your light. Help me to tell you my whole story that I may be healed. Lord, thank you for loving me. Thank you for calling me back to you. In Jesus' name I pray. Amen.

About the Writer

Clesha Staten is a teller of biblical stories and an ordained minister residing in Philadelphia. She has developed the interactive online community In Your Secret Place, which teaches people how to "exhale, relax, and listen" so they can hear God's voice over the chaos that surrounds them—to seek God first and see God in all things. She holds a Master of Divinity from Palmer Theological Seminary of Eastern University and is a member of the Network of Biblical Storytellers. She travels to churches in the tri-state area sharing the Good News through dramatic telling of God's stories.

2

Bent-Over Woman

Set Free to Stand Tall

KIMBERLY DYBECK

> *Healing doesn't always happen in an instant,*
> *but in an instant it can happen!*

Hook Question

How would you respond if Jesus healed you from what has been crippling you?

Biblical Story

LUKE 13:10-13

Now he was teaching in one of the synagogues on the Sabbath. And just then there appeared a woman with a spirit that had crippled her for eighteen years. She was bent over and was quite unable to stand up straight. When Jesus saw her, he called her over and said, "Woman, you are set free from your ailment." When he laid his hands on her, immediately she stood up straight and began praising God.

Biblical Exposition

Meet an ancient woman who had an encounter with Jesus. The details about her are vague, but we know this: her body had some type of affliction that made it impossible for her to stand up straight. Perhaps the woman in this story was not much older than the eighteen years she had experienced this disability. Maybe she had a crippling accident as a child. Had she wandered in the path of some large animal in the ancient streets? Or had her first-century parents searched unsuccessfully to find a cure for a childhood ailment that left their otherwise healthy daughter unable to walk upright? Perhaps the woman was older. We may speculate, like Rev. Dr. Barbara Lundblad did in a sermon, that the woman had osteoporosis or that laborious work had caused the condition.[1] Did her body hunch over because of age and the passing of time? We have no details, yet we are assured that her inability to regain her own posture did not hinder Jesus the day she made her way to her house of worship.

We are given no specific name, age, or diagnosis for the woman, but a specific healing came with a word and a touch from Jesus. We aren't told what she said before arriving at the synagogue, but her legacy reads that she began praising God after Jesus healed her spirit and her body. Her spirit seemed to gain an upright posture to match the posture of her healed back! Eighteen long, painful years—they were not erased with her healing, but her story, like ours, held a turning point the moment she encountered Jesus.

Answers to this woman's prayers may seem to have been delayed, but one day when the woman did not expect it, she received a surprise! She made no audible request of Jesus that day, but Jesus saw her and undertook her healing. Eighteen years! Can you imagine how life changed for her after that unexpected encounter? I can!

Personal Story

I, too, was bent over—not physically, but in every other way. When I was a young mother with three small children, my husband abandoned me. My reserve of hope dwindled like my sparse bank account. My husband's words and actions made clear that reconciliation was not on our horizon. This cruel reality crippled my spirit in pain. His physical departure from our home was a continuation of the spiritual and emotional distancing that had been moving him closer to the lifestyle he desired and further from the one I imagined. Our opportunity to discover the depths of covenant love was cut short by his abandoning me.

I felt discarded like a piece of trash, and it seemed as if the future suddenly vanished and all I could see was the ground! The further I hung my head in shame and sadness, the more my husband seemed to take delight. My emotions, my spirit, and eventually my body sank under the pressure. The negative messages aimed at hurting me struck like physical blows.

Sometimes I felt the physical blows too. The first time was a shock. My husband's steel-tipped boot sank into my stomach with such force that I bent in half, holding my stomach until the pain subsided. From that position I could see the back of his legs heading out the door before it slammed shut, leaving me with his demeaning words echoing in my head. That was the first time. Many years passed, almost as many as the bent-over woman in Luke's Gospel waited to be free from whatever crippled her.

For my three little boys and me, surviving those years was sometimes like being tossed unexpectedly into the turbulent waters of violent rapids. We felt the impact of being swept further and further away from any sense of security, safety, or peace. Hope of being an intact family was all but snuffed out. Like the woman in Luke's Gospel who attended her house of worship bent over year after year, I attended my house of worship with a broken heart and a crippled life.

Blame will bend us over. When my husband left, he told me it was my fault and cast the full weight and responsibility of his leaving on me. Carrying those words around bent me over in my spirit. Intimidation kept me looking down.

Confusion will bend us over. Shallow words of love and admiration stuck in me like a hook, even when my husband's actions said he did not love me or value what we had agreed was valuable. He wanted freedom to do what he wanted with whom he wanted, and sometimes I was on the list of things desired. The pressure of discovering reality in his mixed messages left me no strength to feel anything but mentally and emotionally bent over.

Wondering—replaying interactions over and over to try to understand—will bend us over. Wondering can bend thoughts so significantly that we seek mercy from one with no mercy, and the effect is so dizzying that standing upright becomes impossible.

My sons were growing up. Fear, financial worries, and health issues began to consume my days. Doubt that God would protect and heal us became especially challenging when cancer tests, operations, and finally ulcerative colitis physically bent me in half at times.

I talked to God constantly about our sons. I left room in my heart for my husband to return beyond what everyone thought reasonable because I knew God could heal anything. Living so long apart from the vitality of life that God created us for was a struggle, and I had to face the fact that I no longer held the vision I once had of what healing would look like.

I avoided pain by avoiding sleeping in our bedroom until one day a friend encouraged me to make the room my own. When no one was home, I got to work! In the process, I found the box with my wedding gown and veil that had been under the bed. I pulled out the dress and collapsed on the floor in a heap of beautiful white. I wept from a place deep inside of me, soaking my gown in tears. I do not know how long I was facedown with nothing between me and the floor but my gown, but I remember the moment I heard a kind voice telling me to lift up my head. What happened next transformed my life.

Raising my eyes just a little, I saw a man's feet in sandals just beyond the hem of my wedding dress. I followed the robe with my eyes until I felt the touch of a hand under my chin and heard the words, "Daughter, *lift up your head*; you are mine. You are not abandoned by me." As I stood, other words were imparted somehow, and I was draped in peace. We laughed. I knew the love and peace that filled me was not of my own imagination, and I could only dance around thanking and loving God for visiting me. My spirit healed first, and for the first time in years, I stood up straight! My life has been different since that day. I know I am loved, beautiful to God, never abandoned, and created for purpose. And I do not have to fear the future for my precious children!

I won't say it did not take time to adjust to the view. Standing upright after being bent over so long was quite a transition. Like the bent-over woman who went to the synagogue year after year until one day in about the eighteenth year of her infirmity, Jesus surprised her, Jesus surprised me too.

We never know when or how God will intervene, but we can know for certain that God will be freeing and healing and straightening out those Satan has bent. The woman in Luke did not have to beg. Jesus saw her and he called her over to him and said, "Woman, you are set free from your ailment." What is ailing you? "Daughter, lift up your head!"

Questions

1. Even though we may not walk around physically bent over, what issues in our culture cause people to feel bent over? What causes you to feel bent over?
2. What areas of life are affected negatively when our spirit is bent low?
3. What adjustments would you have to make if you were free to lift your head and stand upright again?
4. How would you respond to this type of unexpected healing in your life?

Thought for Your Day

It is never too late to be surprised by what God will do.

Closing Prayer

God, you know the spirits that bind us, and you see the things that wear us down. Help us to be faithful to continue our walk with you, and teach us all that you would have us learn in every season of life. Thank you for never abandoning us. Straighten us up when we are broken and bent over, so that we may praise you and be a living testimony of your healing power. Amen.

About the Writer

Kimberly Dybeck received her Master of Divinity from Palmer Theological Seminary of Eastern University. Kimberly offers pastoral care as a hospital chaplain. She received her clinical pastoral education and training for chaplaincy from Nemours Alfred I. duPont Hospital for Children in Wilmington, Delaware. She is a creative teacher and biblical storyteller who often uses her own mixed-media art, original songs, and poetry to share messages of faith.

NOTES

1. Rev. Dr. Barbara K. Lundblad, "Healing the Infirmity of Spirit," 30 Good Minutes, Chicago Sunday Evening Club, Program 5308, February 11, 2013, www.30goodminutes.org.

3

Peter's Mother-in-Law

Set Free to Serve

ANGELINE L. WASHINGTON-CLARK

> *It's not about you.*

Hook Question

Where do you see God performing miracles in the world around you today?

Biblical Story

MATTHEW 8:14-17

When Jesus entered Peter's house, he saw his mother-in-law lying in bed with a fever; he touched her hand, and the fever left her, and she got up and began to serve him. That evening they brought to him many who were possessed by demons; and he cast out the spirits with a word, and cured all who were sick. This was to fulfill what had been spoken through the prophet Isaiah, "He took our infirmities and bore our diseases."

Biblical Exposition

Matthew 8 is about some of Christ's miracles, including the healing of a leper, a centurion's servant, and (the focus of our study) Simon Peter's mother-in-law. In Matthew's telling, Jesus cured Peter's mother-in-law of fever, as captured concisely in verses 14-15. The Lord simply touched her hand to heal her.

The same story is captured in the first chapter of the Gospel of Mark, verse 30-31: "Now Simon's mother-in-law was in bed with a fever, and they told him about her at once. He came and took her by the hand and lifted her up. Then the fever left her, and she began to serve them."

Luke also tells the story: "After leaving the synagogue he entered Simon's house. Now Simon's mother-in-law was suffering from a high fever, and they asked him about her. Then he stood over her and rebuked the fever, and it left her. Immediately she got up and began to serve them" (4:38-39). The difference in Luke's account is that Jesus "rebuked" the fever, and no mention is made of him touching her. He used only words to exercise his authority to heal.

As Christians, when we accept Jesus Christ as our personal Lord and Savior, we have that same power through touch and that same authority through words to exercise by faith against evil.

In each of the Gospels, the entire encounter is covered in just two verses, but even in the scarce details, we can determine that Simon Peter was married and that his wife's mother was living among his family. (That there is no mention of his wife may suggest that she had died, perhaps in childbirth or even of the same illness that afflicted her mother.)

Simon Peter's mother-in-law received healing from God, which was a miracle. Dictionary.com defines a miracle as "an effect or event manifesting or considered as a work of God."[1] This effect or extraordinary event in the physical world that surpasses all known human or natural powers is unexplainable and not usually understood by the human mind. David Holwerda, in *Jesus and Israel*, reminds us that "cleanliness, forgiveness, and healing formerly received through the symbolism of ritual law and temple sacrifice are now gifts of Jesus' word and healing touch."[2] According to God's Word,

Jesus has the power to perform miracles, just as he did when he touched Peter's mother-in-law. Therefore, no one should be surprised to learn about the miracle of God's healing power, nor should anyone be surprised by the miracles God continues to perform in the lives of those called to serve.

After she was healed, Peter's mother-in-law immediately began to serve Jesus and those with him. Alan Richardson observes in the *Miracle Stories of the Gospels*, "Christians who have been delivered from the power of sin and restored to health should at once begin to use their blessings in the service of the Lord."[3] Those who have been recipients of God's love and power have a responsibility to share that same love and power with everyone they encounter.

Personal Story

On January 24, 2011, while I was driving to Perryville, Maryland, to catch a commuter train headed to Washington, DC, God touched me with a miracle. On the previous day, I learned of anticipated inclement weather that was headed north, and that same night I dreamed of having a weather-related car accident. But when I awoke the next morning and looked out the window and saw that the day was clear, I prepared to travel. The train station is approximately sixty miles from my home, and approximately twenty miles into the trip, I received a phone call from a friend who begged me to turn around and return to Philadelphia. She had learned that the impending storm was coming from the south, but I tried to assure her that the roads were dry, I was safe, and I could make it to work.

What happened next still feels like a dream. While driving south on I-95 at just before five o'clock in the morning, I suddenly drove into what seemed like a void. I had entered a whiteout—"a polar weather condition caused by a heavy cloud cover over the snow, in which the light coming from above is approximately equal to the light reflected from below, and which is characterized by absence of shadow, invisibility of the horizon, and discernibility of only very dark objects."[4] I could not see anything but darkness. I was blinded and unable to see even to pull over or exit the highway.

The next thing I recall was a tractor trailer driving around my car, and once it was in front of me, I could see its red taillights. At that moment, I prayed aloud and asked for God's help, forgiveness, mercy, and grace. And then it was as if I visually entered into a movie. Although I was awake and struggling to see what was ahead of my car, I was able to see images of my life ending. In front of me were pictures of my car crashing, and then I seemed to see myself dead inside the car. As the movie continued to play in my mind's eye, I saw images of my mother standing over my body on the highway, and I could hear her scream, which caused me to pray louder.

Then I saw images of my funeral, and in one scene it appeared that my six-year-old niece, dressed beautifully for the occasion, was being picked up to kiss me in the casket. God seemed to be showing me images of what could occur in my life even as I drove down the highway, as if the Lord wanted to demonstrate complete authority over all things and the power to save life. Right then I screamed and surrendered to God.

As I continued to drive for what seemed like forever, the female voice of the navigation system came through the speakers and said, "You are one mile from your destination on the right."

It was a miracle that I did not crash. It was a miracle that I did not die. It was a miracle that God had one hand on the car and the other on me, leading me off the highway safely to my destination. When I finally got to the office and opened the door, the phone rang, and it was my mother. She asked, "Are, you okay? I woke up around five o'clock and heard myself praying for you and became worried but was afraid to call."

What she did not know was that at five o'clock, I had been in between life and death, and God had rebuked the death angel who was hovering over my car. My mother, unaware of my circumstances and miles away, had joined my prayers, asking God for help, just as Simon Peter had asked Jesus to help his wife's mother.

My mother's last words on the phone that morning, which were, "Angeline, God is calling you but you have to answer because God has plans that include you," placed me on the path to fully and completely serve the Lord. God's healing power saved me on that road, not simply to tell this story but also to serve God's people.

Questions

1. What story do you have to tell of Jesus performing a miracle in your life?
2. How has Jesus' healing power set you (or someone you know) free in order to serve?
3. In what ways do you have authority over the "fever" in your life?
4. How do you see your role as a servant in the body of Christ?

Thought for Your Day

God is calling everyone to serve, but you have to pay attention and answer the call.

Closing Prayer

God, in the name of Jesus, we love you and thank you for your healing power and for calling us into service for you. We thank you for all that you have done, and we ask that you forgive us for not recognizing your power in all that we are and do. Thank you for saving us so that we can do your will, and most of all, thank you for your Son, Jesus. Please help us to know that each one of us is a miracle that you saved for service. We love you and praise you and thank you in the precious name of Jesus and for his sake. Amen.

About the Writer

Angeline L. Washington-Clark is an entrepreneur, inspirational speaker, and social change agent devoted to teaching, mentoring, and coaching people of all ages toward a better life. She uses her passion for education to inspire and challenge people to be their best. Angeline is an active member at Enon Tabernacle Baptist Church in Philadelphia, Pennsylvania, and works as a budget manager for the United States federal government in Washington, DC. She is currently completing dual master's degrees, in divinity and in international development, from Palmer Theological Seminary at Eastern University.

NOTES

1. S.v. "miracle," Dictionary.com, http://dictionary.reference.com/browse/miracle?s=t.

2. David E. Holwerda, *Jesus and Israel: One Covenant or Two?* (Grand Rapids: Eerdmans, 1995), 69.

3. Alan Richardson, *The Miracle Stories of the Gospel* (1941; repr., London: SCM, 1952), 76.

4. S.v., "whiteout," The Free Dictionary.com, www.thefreedictionary.com/white+out.

Part 2

Women Who Risked in Faith

4

Woman with the Alabaster Jar

Risking Extravagant Love

JACQUELINE WILSON-DANDROW

> *Being deeply loved by someone gives you strength,*
> *while loving someone deeply gives you courage.*
> —LAO TZU
>
> *I have decided to stick with love.*
> *Hate is too great a burden to bear.*
> —MARTIN LUTHER KING, JR.

Hook Question

What would you risk to turn your secret mourning into joy (Isaiah 61:3)?

Biblical Story

LUKE 7:36-50

One of the Pharisees asked Jesus to eat with him, and he went into the Pharisee's house and took his place at the table. And a woman in the city, who was a sinner, having learned that he was eating in the Pharisee's house, brought an alabaster jar of ointment. She stood behind him at his feet, weeping, and began to bathe his feet with her tears and to dry them with her hair. Then she continued kissing his feet and anointing them with the ointment. Now when the Pharisee who had invited him saw it, he said to himself, "If this man were a prophet, he would have known who and what kind of woman that is who is touching him—that she is a sinner. Jesus spoke up and said to him, "Simon, I have something to say to you." "Teacher," he replied, "speak." "A certain creditor had two debtors; one owed five hundred denarii, and the other fifty. When they could not pay, he canceled the debts for both of them. Now which of them will love him more?" Simon answered, "I supposed the one for whom he canceled the greater debt." And Jesus said to him, "You have judged rightly." Then turning toward the woman, he said to Simon, "Do you see this woman? I entered your house; you gave me no water for my feet, but she has bathed my feet with her tears and dried them with her hair. You gave me no kiss, but from the time I came in she has not stopped kissing my feet. You did not anoint my head with oil, but she has anointed my feet with ointment. Therefore, I tell you, her sins, which were many, have been forgiven; hence she has shown great love. But the one to whom little is forgiven, loves little." Then he said to her, "Your sins are forgiven." But those who were at the table with him began to say among themselves, "Who is this who even forgives sins?" And he said to the woman, "Your faith has saved you; go in peace."

Biblical Exposition

The woman in this story was the shame and disgrace of the community, of her family, and of herself. Although we do not know the kind of life this woman led or what happened in her past that made others treat her with such indignation and disgust, we do know that her sins were many. Whatever her sins, they made her an outcast among the people and the Pharisees, who believed that to walk in holiness, people must physically separate themselves from sin and sinners. This woman's sins were well known, as was revealed in the words of Simon the Pharisee.

At some point, this woman must have heard the Lord's teachings on the forgiveness of sins, and on love, compassion, and hope, because she came to Christ seeking with all her heart for forgiveness of her sins and for the love and compassion of the Savior. She was driven to bring an end to the oppression, ridicule, and condemnation that was thrust on her by people. Her secret mourning for the loss of honor, respect, virtue, relationship, and especially love drove her with great determination to push her way through to Christ. Against all odds and opposition, through sneers and comments of condemnation, she did not even pause, but ran to Christ. For she knew she would receive forgiveness and comfort for all that she mourned. She knew Jesus would give her beauty for her ashes and the oil of joy for what she mourned.

When I think of this woman, I always wonder what she lived through. Did she mourn the loss of innocence that was stolen from her when she was a child? Could she have been sodomized or raped and left to mourn this stolen innocence? Was she put down, degraded, rejected, or told she would never amount to anything and left to deal with the loss of self-esteem, never understanding how precious and beautiful she was in God's eyes? Maybe someone told her that no one would ever want her because she was ugly, overweight, or stupid. Or maybe she was an orphan and never had anyone who loved her or showed her love or what it was to love one's self. When I think of this woman, I always wonder what her story really was.

Personal Story

My parents were not affectionate people. They did not show affection toward one another or toward my siblings and me, but I was a child who longed for a hug, a kiss, a hand to hold, or a shoulder to cry on. Without such displays from my immediate family, I began to look for affection from whoever was willing to give it.

By the time I became a teenager, I was still looking for love and affection. That was when I subconsciously began to believe sex was love. This conclusion was a result of observing how men seemed to offer romance and affection when the possibility of a physical relationship was involved. Sexual intimacy seemed to be what made men love you. At age fifteen, I started seeing this man who was thirty or thirty-five years old. We would sneak around to see each other; most of the time we would go to different hotels, but occasionally we would go to his house. I imagine that most people thought I was his daughter. All I know was that in my mind he adored me.

At age eighteen I stopped seeing the older man because I met the man I loved and married. A couple of years into the marriage, I found out he was on drugs. I caught him one day shooting up in the bathroom. Of course he said it was his first time, but I knew that was a lie. In the two years we had been married, he was constantly selling everything in the house— including the food I would buy. I would put it in the freezer, and the next morning it would be gone. I knew something was wrong, but until I caught him doing the drugs, I did not know what it was.

I hung in there with him for a few years after that incident, supporting him while he went in and out of rehab and bailing him out of jail when he got caught doing whatever it was he was doing out there in the street. I hung in there until he started showing signs of violence. He had hit me once before we got married, but I thought I had deserved it, so of course, I forgave him, and it didn't happen again.

Then one day over dinner, he and I began to argue. He got angry and threw a plate against the wall. Another time I was upstairs and my son came running up crying with grape jelly on his face; he told me his father had thrown the sandwich at him. I knew at that point I was going to leave.

I guess he knew it too, because he began to threaten me. He told me there was no place I could go where he would not find me. One day after he left the house, I took the kids and ran to my parents' house. He began to stalk me. I went to the police and got a restraining order. He continued to stalk me no matter where I went. I called the police; sometimes they would catch him, but all they would do is tell him to leave. Then, after they left, he would come back.

A few times he caught me and beat me up. I called the police, but again they were no help. Eventually I moved back in with my parents. My husband continued to stalk me despite the restraining order. Finally, I told myself, *There is no way out of this. No one can protect me! I have to deal with him myself.*

I plotted to kill my husband. I believed that if I did not kill him, eventually he would kill me. He had always told me that if I left him again, he would find me and kill me.

One day I was sitting in my parents' house making a plan in my head about what I was going to do and how I was going to do it. I was thinking about where I was going to go to get the gun, when my father walked in and said to me out of the clear blue sky, "Jackie, that man is not worth going to jail for." Too shocked to respond, I just looked at him, and he walked away.

So I gave up my plan to kill the man. Instead, I left my parents' home again, sneaking away in the middle of the night with my sons without telling anyone where we were going.

I wish I could say that after all of this—after escaping—I went on to create a life for my children and myself that was full of joy and happiness, but that was not the case. It was lonely and heartbreaking because I did not know anyone and I could not reach out to my friends and family. It was the first time in my life I was on my own, not because I wanted to be, but because I had to be. I lived in the fear that someone would see me and say something that would get back to my husband and he would find out where we were, so I looked over my shoulder a lot. But I pushed forward, looking for a job, getting my sons situated in school, trying to get familiar with the area without bringing attention to us, doing whatever was necessary to keep us safe.

At that time I was not walking in faith. I was doing whatever I had to do in order to survive, probably much like the biblical woman with the alabaster box. I am sure she was doing whatever she had to do in order to survive. Surely she was focused on what needed to be done and not on what was being done to her. Not until she met the Lord and experienced deliverance at his hands and kindness in his words did she move from survival to a walk of faith.

Like her, not until I turned to the Lord many years later did I come to understand that God was with me and had sustained me through it all. In hindsight I came to understand that the Lord loved me and always watched over me. This is why I completely relate to this woman who was compelled and determined, no matter the cost, to push through whatever she had to in order to reach Christ. Knowing that through all the craziness of your life God is loving you, protecting you, standing with you, and watching over you—that knowledge compels you to risk whatever you have to, in order to get to Jesus.

Mine was a long and painful journey, but I've come to believe that every negative thing that happened in my life caused me to seek a greater purpose and power. It led me back to God—even if my return to Christ did take more than fourteen years. I say I returned to God because I knew Christ as a child. I met him in Sunday school when I was very young, and when I was younger, Christ was with me. He used to talk with me, and I used to talk with him. My parents did not believe this kind of thing was possible, so they began to call me weird. Because of their ridicule of my faith, I walked away from the Lord. I did not want to be strange anymore. So, not knowing any better, instead of running to God, I ran away from the Lord.

I understand the force that drove the woman with her alabaster jar to seek out and find the Lord. I understand the power of love that allowed her to risk everything to express her gratitude in such an extravagant way. I know the great strength and determination that came out of the depths of her soul, compelling her to claw her way out of self-destructive grief and a loss of self to nurture a mustard seed of faith found in the living Word of God.

This woman who loved much, the woman with the alabaster jar—I know her well. I know this woman because I am this woman.

Questions

1. What have you experienced in your life that drove you to the feet of Christ? What did you expect to find at the Lord's feet and why?
2. Jesus compared the lack of hospitality Simon offered to the extravagant hospitality the woman gave. What are the rules of hospitality in your life? What would an extravagant welcome look like today?
3. When have you received or given an extravagant act of love? How did it make you feel?
4. Remembering Jesus' comments about how one who has been forgiven much, loves much, do you believe it is harder to love if you have not first experienced forgiveness? Why or why not?

Thought for Your Day

"Guard me as the apple of the eye; hide me in the shadow of your wings" (Psalm 17:8).

Closing Prayer

Most gracious and merciful God, blessed are you and blessed is your holy name. Let me thank you first, Lord, for your mighty and majestic love, your loving-kindness and unmerited favor. You have looked upon me and had compassion on me. You have taken me in your loving arms to protect and comfort me and have hidden me in the shadow of your wings. Even as the enemy seeks to kill, steal, and destroy that which is within me, I know you are my rock, my fortress, my deliverer, and my rescuer in the time of need. You are the God of my strength, and I will trust in you. In all things, I look to you, for I know there is no tribulation, distress, persecution, famine, nakedness, peril, sword, height, depth, or any creature that shall be able to separate the love of God from me, which is in my Lord and Savior Christ Jesus. I give you all honor and all praise in the name of Jesus. Amen.

About the Writer

Jacqueline Wilson-Dandrow is a student at Palmer Theological Seminary, where she is completing her Master of Divinity. Her goals upon completing her degree are to continue her education through a chaplain residency program, become a member of the Association for Professional Chaplains, and become board certified as a chaplain through the Board of Chaplaincy Certification Inc.

5

Ruth

Devotion for the Long Haul

LORI MITCHELL

> *Still, without faithfulness of heart there is little value
> in all the rest.*
> —DeAnna Julie Dodson

Hook Question

To whom in this life are you faithfully dedicated?

Biblical Story

RUTH 1:1-18

In the days when the judges ruled, there was a famine in the
land, and a certain man of Bethlehem in Judah went to live
in the country of Moab, he and his wife and two sons. The
name of the man was Elimelech and the name of his wife
Naomi, and the names of his two sons were Mahlon and
Chilion; they were Ephrathites from Bethlehem in Judah.
They went into the country of Moab and remained there.
But Elimelech, the husband of Naomi, died, and she was left
with her two sons. These took Moabite wives; the name of
the one was Orpah and the name of the other Ruth. When

they had lived there about ten years, both Mahlon and Chilion also died, so that the woman was left without her two sons and her husband. Then she started to return with her daughters-in-law from the country of Moab, for she had heard in the country of Moab that the LORD had considered his people and given them food. So she set out from the place where she had been living, she and her two daughters-in-law, and they went on their way to go back to the land of Judah. But Naomi said to her two daughters-in-law, "Go back each of you to your mother's house. May the LORD deal kindly with you, as you have dealt with the dead and with me. The LORD grant that you may find security, each of you in the house of your husband." Then she kissed them, and they wept aloud. They said to her, "No, we will return with you to your people." But Naomi said, "Turn back, my daughters, why will you go with me? Do I still have sons in my womb that they may become your husbands? Turn back, my daughters, go your way, for I am too old to have a husband. Even if I thought there was hope for me, even if I should have a husband tonight and bear sons, would you then wait until they were grown? Would you then refrain from marrying? No, my daughters, it has been far more bitter for me than for you, because the hand of the LORD has turned against me." Then they wept aloud again. Orpah kissed her mother-in-law, but Ruth clung to her.

So she said, "See, your sister-in-law has gone back to her people and to her gods; return after your sister-in-law." But Ruth said,

> "Do not press me to leave you
> or to turn back from following you!
> Where you go, I will go;
> where you lodge, I will lodge;
> your people shall be my people,
> and your God my God.
> Where you die, I will die—
> there will I be buried.

> May the LORD do thus and so to me,
>   and more as well,
> if even death parts me from you!"

When Naomi saw that she was determined to go with her, she said no more to her.

Biblical Exposition

The book of Ruth opens with a Jewish family suffering from many problems. Famine in Bethlehem forces the family of Elimelech and Naomi, his wife, to head toward Moab with their sons in search of food; they remained there for around ten years. While there, the sons of Elimelech and Naomi married two local girls, Orpah and Ruth. The life of the family was happily going along when, one by one, Naomi's husband and two sons died. This tragedy left the three women husbandless and vulnerable in a society where women were valued only in relationship to a man. Naomi decided to move back to Bethlehem, and her daughters-in-law wanted to follow her. Naomi urged them to stay behind, and while Orpah was convinced to go back home, Ruth refused to turn back, saying, "Do not press me to leave you or to turn back from following you! Where you go, I will go; where you lodge, I will lodge; your people shall be my people, and your God my God" (Ruth 1:16).

Faithfulness is the key theme of the book of Ruth. Ruth exemplifies faithfulness in her relationships with her mother-in-law, Naomi; Boaz; and God. The Hebrew word for faithfulness, *hesed*, which can be translated as "loving-kindness" and indicates loyalty, is woven throughout the book of Ruth, beginning in chapter 1, verse 8. Both Ruth and Boaz exhibit *hesed* to their family members throughout the story. These are not acts of kindness with an expectation; they are acts of *hesed* that demonstrate that a person can go beyond the minimum required out of covenant loyalty. In return for this faithfulness, God rewarded Ruth by making her part of Israel's royal family when her son Obed became the father of Jesse, who became the father of King David. Ruth is full of faithfulness and kindness toward everyone.

In this story, various characters show selfless love toward others, which God expects from the people of God. A high sense of honor also dominates the book of Ruth. The women are particularly honorable and hardworking. Boaz treats Ruth with great honor and respect, while fulfilling his legal and familial responsibilities. Moreover, the book demonstrates commitment. Ruth shows her devotion by taking care of Naomi, her mother-in-law. In turn, Naomi looks after her daughter-in-law Ruth. And eventually God, through Boaz, secures a future and the family line for Naomi and Ruth. Lastly, God takes care of all and blesses Ruth and Boaz with a child.

Personal Story

At 7:30 on the night of my birthday, the phone rang. *Is it someone to wish me a happy birthday?* I wondered. My happiness was quickly replaced with fear. My father was on the other end of the line, calling to see if I had seen my mother at all that day. It turns out she had left their house around dinnertime and was missing. Little did I know that my night was just beginning to unfold.

Nine o'clock rolled around, then ten. Should I go look for her? Should I call the police? I feverishly prayed for wisdom and safety for my mother. Then my dad called back to let me know that he was going to bed. To bed! How could he sleep?

By then my mother had been gone for more than six hours. I began to gather her information together, realizing that I did not even have her car's license plate number. My parents live a distance away from me and out in the country, so I would have to call the state police. Would my dad get mad if I called the police?

Suddenly my husband came into the room with his cellphone in hand. He gave me the phone. "It's an EMT." My heart started racing. Was my mom okay?

The EMT explained that my mother had seemed confused when she pulled into a tollbooth and asked directions to their little country town. She was three counties away from home. He was going to take her to the hospital. I must go to the hospital to get her.

I made the trek to the emergency room and sat with my mother while the hospital staff ran tests. The doctor inquired, "Is she usually this confused?" I assured them that this was unfortunately a new normal reality for her. I patiently waited with her. I asked her, "Where were you headed?" She was going out to get me a birthday cake. For four hours, we lingered there. After a CT scan and many sticks for blood work, I was able to take her home.

This is just part of my life's saga since my mother started struggling with mental illness and dementia. At first I was in denial; after all, it was not my problem. I had school, a husband, and ministry things to take care of. But I soon made a decision that I needed to step up and be proactive in her life. My mother deserved that.

Now our roles have changed. Sometimes I must tell her to take a bath, remind her of the date, brush her hair. I have shed many tears for the mother I feel I no longer have, but I also have determination to help my mother live a life full of dignity. I listen to her and make her comfortable because regardless, family sticks together.

Like Ruth, I find family important. And like Ruth, I will not let my mother's illness leave me behind. I journey with her into the future. No matter how confusing or frustrating life with dementia may be, we will work through it together. Following Ruth's example of faithfulness, I believe I can provide stability, security, and confidence for my mother and family. My life with her will reflect in some small way the faithfulness of God to others. My relationship with my mom helps me to have a faithful heart that keeps me in a close walk with God.

Faithfulness is a fruit of the Spirit, empowered by God. So I will pray for it. Model it. Teach it. Celebrate it. This can be your prayer too.

Questions

1. Ruth's choice to remain by Naomi's side necessitated moving away from her past. When have you made a breach with some facet of your past? What were the effects of that decision?
2. Naomi lost her husband and sons. Describe a time where you felt loss in your life. Did you reveal those feelings to anyone? Did you communicate your hurt with God? Why or why not?
3. How hard is it for you, like Ruth, to be there to journey with others when all you can do is wait with them for the deliverance that only God can give? Which of your present relationships may necessitate this type of restraint?

Thought for Your Day

Your faithfulness makes you trustworthy to God.[1]

Closing Prayer

Lord, help me improve my understanding, and encourage me to do what you ask me to do. Assist me in being faithful to journey with others as I follow you. Amen.

About the Writer

Lori Mitchell, a native of southern New Jersey, is a graduate of Eastern University and a Master of Divinity candidate at Palmer Theological Seminary. Lori is pastoring and doing youth ministry in the United Methodist Church. She and her husband, Dan, have been married for fifteen years.

NOTE

1. Edwin Louis Cole quotes, BrainyQuote.com, www.brainyquote.com/quotes/quotes/e/edwinlouis360143.html.

6

Rahab

Believe In and Rely On the Promises of God

DAVID GAINES

> By faith Rahab the prostitute did not perish with those
> who were disobedient, because she had received the
> spies in peace.
> —HEBREWS 11:31

Hook Question

How does faith in a promise help someone to gain victory?

Biblical Story

JOSHUA 2:12-21

"Now then, since I have dealt kindly with you, swear to me
by the LORD that you in turn will deal kindly with my family.
Give me a sign of good faith that you will spare my father and
mother, my brothers and sisters, and all who belong to them,
and deliver our lives from death." The men said to her, "Our
life for yours! If you do not tell this business of ours, then we
will deal kindly and faithfully with you when the LORD gives
us the land."

Then she let them down by a rope through the window,
for her house was on the outer side of the city wall and she
resided within the wall itself. She said to them, "Go toward

the hill country, so that the pursuers may not come upon you. Hide yourselves there three days, until the pursuers have returned; then afterward you may go your way." The men said to her, "We will be released from this oath that you have made us swear to you if we invade the land and you do not tie this crimson cord in the window through which you let us down, and you do not gather into your house your father and mother, your brothers, and all your family. If any of you go out of the doors of your house into the street, they shall be responsible for their own death, and we shall be innocent; but if a hand is laid upon any who are with you in the house, we shall bear the responsibility for their death. But if you tell this business of ours, then we shall be released from this oath that you made us swear to you." She said, "According to your words, so be it." She sent them away and they departed. Then she tied the crimson cord in the window.

Biblical Exposition

Jericho was a highly protected city due to its massive fortification from the walls that surrounded the city. The retaining wall was some thirteen to sixteen feet high. On top of that was a mud brick wall six and a half feet thick and about twenty-six to thirty-two feet high. At the crest of the embankment was a similar mud brick wall whose base was roughly forty-six feet above the ground level outside the retaining wall.

The city of Jericho represented a daunting obstacle to Israel's claim of the Promised Land. Even after God assured Joshua that victory over the apparently unassailable walled city would be theirs, the people of Israel were frightened. Even Joshua chose to send spies to scope out the situation before implementing the strategy provided by the Lord.

While some scholars and church tradition have offered various rationales for the total destruction of Jericho, ranging from wickedness to rival Sodom and Gomorrah to temple prostitution and wide-ranging sexual immorality to more garden-variety charges of idolatry, the narrative in Judges offers little by way of moral justification. Certainly the people of the city were not worshipers of the Lord God of Israel. That alone made them spiritual enemies and a territorial obstacle to Israel's settlement in the Promised Land.

Thus, the true God of Israel gave the power to God's people to destroy the walls of Jericho and commit each person within the city walls to the edge of the sword except for Rahab and her family, according to the promise made between her and the Israelite spies. The only conditions were that Rahab trust the spies and put a red crimson cord in her window and that Rahab's family trust her and remain in her house during the invasion.

Personal Story

Pornography was my idol. While I claimed to worship Jesus, my heart was sold out to lusting after women I have never met. One exposure to pornography led to a deep, long, downhill spiral into illicit sexual conduct. I felt like I was alone in my sin until some of my friends in the faith confessed that they struggled with this same problem. I remember my brother told me that an addiction to pornography was like an addiction to drugs, and his statement rang true for me.

Pornography was not only my god, but it was also my "functional savior." Whenever I was stressed out, upset, angry, disappointed, feeling like a failure, and lonely, I always had a friend in pornography. What I did not know was that the more I entrusted myself to pornography, the more pornography wanted of me. It consumed my time, thoughts, desires, relationships, and ultimately my relationship with the real God, Jesus Christ. I found myself desiring and choosing to spend time viewing pornography rather than to be with my friends. The worst part about viewing pornography was that while I was learning more about Jesus, getting a theological education at the master's level, and teaching a Bible study, I was living as a hypocrite. I would talk about the faith I had in Jesus Christ yet engage in secret sin privately. I felt like there was no hope for me and that this is who I would be for all the days of my life.

One day the Lord showed me, through a book written by Dr. John Piper called *Battling Unbelief*, that it is possible to overcome the sin of using pornography. He mentioned that "the fire of lust's pleasures must be fought with the fire of God's pleasures."[1] This meant that I needed to rely on the promises of God found in Scripture by faith.

Rahab set a prime example for me as to what I needed to do to overcome my struggle with sin—and her checkered past as a prostitute seemed to offer both empathy and hope as a role model for me. Faith was the key to Rahab's deliverance from Israel's invasion when the Israelite army was ready to invade the city of Jericho. The promise given to her by the spies proved to be exactly what she needed to be delivered from the pursuing Israelites. This promise is described in Joshua 2:12, where Rahab asks for a "sign of good faith" from the two spies as remuneration for hiding them from the people of Jericho. She describes what she wants in the following verse: "You will spare my father and mother, my brothers and sisters, and all who belong to them, and deliver our lives from death." The promise made by the spies was not just a promise between them and Rahab, but also by God to Rahab. This is made evident by God instructing Joshua and the Israelites to spare Rahab and her family during their invasion of Jericho in Joshua 6. The promise was like the door leading to Rahab's exit, but her faith in the promise was the key to opening that door.

Rahab ultimately had two ways to respond to the spies' promise. She could have doubted the promise given to her by the spies and perished with the city or believed the promise and followed the instructions given to her. It is clear that she believed the promise, because her faith led to action as she tied the crimson cord in her window (v. 21). This event in history reminds me that my faith, just like Rahab's, will always lead to action. For example, if I doubt God's promises in Scripture, then I will pursue sin, but if I have faith in those promises, then I will pursue Christ. Doubting or having faith in God's promises will dictate the course of action I take. Rahab's faith in God's promise proved to be the victory that saved her, and faith in God's promises have been my victory over sexual sin.

Daily I face the decision, like Rahab, to either disbelieve or believe the promises that I have been given from God. The desire to view pornography can be so strong that it may feel like there is an army prepared to charge against me. Therefore, I have learned, like Rahab, that if I doubt God's promises, I will be destroyed as if by an army invasion, but if I believe God's promises, I will be delivered from death.

Like Rahab, I too have been given several "signs of good faith" from God in which I can put my trust. My favorite promise is found in Psalm 84:10: "For a day in your courts is better than a thousand elsewhere." I must believe that one day of walking in purity and holiness in Christ is better than one thousand days of viewing pornography. I also rely on another promise in 1 Corinthians 10:13: "God is faithful, and he will not let you be tested beyond your strength, but with the testing he will also provide the way out so that you may be able to endure it." If I doubt this truth that God is faithful, then when I am tempted, I will sin, but if I believe God's promise, just as Rahab believed God's promise in Joshua 2, I know I can have victory against any temptation I face. I continue to bank on promises such as these every single day, and I trust God's Word is true.

Through relying on a promise, like Rahab did, I am able to live a life of purity that glorifies Christ Jesus by the power of the Holy Spirit through faith.

Questions

1. How did the spies' promise give hope to Rahab?

2. How do the promises of God found in Scripture give hope to you?
3. What action are you called to take when you begin to rely on the promises of God?

Thought for Your Day

For in [the gospel] the righteousness of God is revealed through faith for faith; as it is written, "The one who is righteous will live by faith" (Romans 1:17).

Closing Prayer

Dear God, thank you for being a great God. Jesus, thank you for providing an excellent example of what faith looks like through the life of Rahab. May we repent of any doubt in our lives toward you and your Word. Help us to rely on your truth and promises revealed through Scripture by the Holy Spirit within us. May we all live a life of faith in Christ Jesus to your glory and our joy. In the only name that can save, Jesus Christ; Amen.

About the Writer

David Gaines is currently a student at Palmer Theological Seminary in King of Prussia, Pennsylvania, pursuing a Master of Theological Studies with a concentration in biblical studies and theology. He is a member of Epiphany Fellowship and works two part-time jobs, as a spinning instructor at LA Fitness and as an ice hockey coach for the Ed Snider Youth Hockey Foundation. He enjoys teaching a Bible study on Thursday evenings at a local Dunkin' Donuts.

NOTE

1. John Piper, *Battling Unbelief: Defeating Sin with Superior Pleasure* (Colorado Springs: Multnomah, 2007), 143.

7

Abigail

What God Has for You Is for You!

STEPHANIE PHILLIPS

> *A soft answer turneth away wrath:*
> *but grievous words stir up anger.*
> —PROVERBS 15:1 (KJV)

Hook Question

When has God used you as a peacemaker?

Biblical Story

1 SAMUEL 25:14-17

But one of the young men told Abigail, Nabal's wife, "David sent messengers out of the wilderness to salute our master; and he shouted insults at them. Yet the men were very good to us, and we suffered no harm, and we never missed anything when we were in the fields, as long as we were with them; they were a wall to us both by night and by day, all the while we were with them keeping the sheep. Now therefore know this and consider what you should do; for evil has been decided against our master and against all his house; he is so ill-natured that no one can speak to him."

Biblical Exposition

Abigail's story takes place after the death of the prophet Samuel, the only one who may have been able to stop Saul from trying to kill David. Saul was king of Israel, and David had been anointed by Samuel to be the next king. David and his servants had taken refuge in the desert from Saul, who was seeking to kill him. A man named Nabal was there shearing his sheep. David sent word to Nabal, asking that food be provided for David and his servants. David also instructed his messengers to speak of the kindness and protection that was shown to Nabal's shepherds by David.

David's request was modest, in keeping with the high value the culture placed on hospitality and reciprocity. Nevertheless, Nabal denied it. Not only did he refuse to return the kindness, but he was verbally abusive to the servants and disrespectful of David. Nabal insisted that the food and drink belonged to him and he was not going to share it with anyone.

David's response was to gather his men so he could destroy Nabal and all that was his. In the meantime, one of Nabal's servants went to Abigail, Nabal's wife, and told her all that had happened. Abigail knew immediately that something must be done to appease David so that her family and household could be saved. Abigail, the peacemaker, rushed to meet David en route with the best food from her pantry. She approached David in a humble, polite, and respectful manner. Can you imagine with me Abigail's thoughts and actions?

> When David and his men came toward me, I got off the donkey and bowed before him. Though taking a chance, I knew I had to speak to him in order to save my household from being destroyed. I asked him to blame me alone for the injustice he suffered and to not take my husband, Nabal, seriously, for he had behaved according to his name—foolishly.
>
> I had heard stories about David, and I knew that God had a great plan for his future. So I blessed David and his future dynasty. I encouraged him

not to take matters into his own hands but to let God mete out justice. If David were to seek revenge, he would shed innocent blood! And God would not be pleased.

David blessed the Lord for sending me to him. Because I acted quickly and with good sense, David blessed me also. I told David that because he had forgiven my trespass, I believed the Lord would establish David's own house and do the good that the prophet had spoken of concerning David. Then I asked David to remember me. David favored me by receiving my gifts and then told me to go in peace.

As I approached my house, I noticed that Nabal was holding a feast, and he was very drunk. I decided to wait until morning to tell him what I had done. When I finally told him the story, he fell to the ground. Medical experts would probably say he had a heart attack. All we know is that ten days later, my husband, the fool, was dead.

When David heard about Nabal's death, he sent his servants to me, asking me to become his wife. Who would have thought I would become the bride of the next king of Israel?

Personal Story

Love can cause people to do strange things. At age nineteen, after completing one year of college, I got married to a man I met while a junior in high school. I was completely head over heels in love. Though we were unequally yoked—I was a Christian and he was not—I felt I had made the right decision. I was determined to change my new spouse for the better. How naïve! As time went on, discussions became arguments when we could not agree on certain values and choices. He did not see the need to change his behaviors, and I could not understand his resistance to my efforts to reform him. Things went from bad to worse in the marriage.

In the meantime, however, God enabled me to finish college and begin teaching at an elementary school in Philadelphia. In that role, God enabled me to be a blessing to the students, staff, and parents by helping people to solve problems in a peaceful manner. And I finally realized that God did not want me to be in a situation filled with stress and unhappiness. I got a divorce and went on with my life, raising my son.

Love was the last thing on my mind. I promised God that I would seek God's guidance and not take things into my own hands this time. Seasons passed, and I soon met a man who was the brother of my next-door neighbor. We became friends, and that friendship developed into love. God had blessed me with someone who was kind, respectful, and God-fearing. We got married and went on to enjoy life. I was not looking for a husband, but God had someone for me. What a blessing! After fourteen years of marriage, he has now gone home to be with the Lord.

In the biblical story, the relationship between Abigail and Nabal was not the best; in fact, it could be seen as an abusive marriage. Yet Abigail remained calm and steadfast as a wife. In the time of this story, women were property and without a voice. Abigail was a brave woman for keeping her plans from her husband and for going to see David by herself. Abigail, knowing the danger of such behavior, did so anyway because she cared for the safety of her family.

I identify with Abigail because I, too, remained in a difficult first marriage—for fourteen years—until it was necessary to end it. My decision to divorce my husband was a difficult one. I felt guilty for not being able to keep my marriage together. How was I going to raise a child by myself? I was raised by a single mother and knew of the sacrifices she made for my well-being. My mother taught me about God and love, which I could give to my child. My faith and compassion also helped me to be an advocate for the children who were in my care as an educator. My relationship with God strengthened me and helped me to overcome many challenges and to do what was necessary.

Abigail's faithfulness to the word of God enabled her to be blessed by God. God orchestrated circumstances, and Abigail was rewarded for her faithfulness. Now she was a widow, but soon she was to become the wife of David. During my life as a single parent, I kept the faith and daily communed with God. There were times when I wanted to give up, but I knew that others depended on me. God then blessed me with another husband and a blessed marriage. God also increased our family with the birth of a daughter.

Questions

1. What does 1 Samuel 25:2-13 tell you about Abigail?
2. What do you learn from Abigail about dealing with a fool like Nabal or an angry person like David?
3. How was Abigail used by God for God's purposes?
4. When in your life have you decided to do something that was wrong but God sent someone or something to stop you?

Thought for Your Day

God can use you for God's glory when you follow God's will.

Closing Prayer

Dear God, we face many challenges as we deal with people and their attitudes in our families, in our communities, and on our jobs. Let us not grow weary in doing good but remember that you are in control and working everything out for good. We praise your name. Amen!

About the Writer

Stephanie Phillips is a retired school educator and principal. She has a love for God and a passion for the people of God, especially youth and young adults. She attended Palmer Theological Seminary of Eastern University. She considers herself to be a lifelong learner.

8

Pontius Pilate's Wife
Speak Out about Your Dreams

JACQUELINE BROWN

> *Expect great things from God;*
> *attempt great things for God.*
> —WILLIAM CAREY

Hook Question

Do you trust God and act on your dreams?

Biblical Story

MATTHEW 27:19
While [Pilate] was sitting on the judgment seat, his wife sent word to him, "Have nothing to do with that innocent man, for today I have suffered a great deal because of a dream about him."

Biblical Exposition

After Judas's betrayal and Jesus' arrest in Gethsemane, Jesus was brought before the Roman governor of Jerusalem. Although Pilate marveled greatly at what Jesus told him, he did not find any legal fault with what Jesus was saying. When

Pilate sat down on the judgment seat (meaning, he was ready to deliver his verdict), his wife sent him a concise but compelling message: "Have nothing to do with that innocent man."

Little to no attention is given to Pilate's wife in the Scriptures. According to Christian legend, her name was Claudia Procula.[1] Her words are found only in the Gospel of Matthew, where she is mentioned in this single verse. Her appearance is brief but dramatic.

Apparently Pilate's wife had lost sleep because of a disturbing dream. No doubt rumors about Jesus and his works had reached the palace. Perhaps she had even seen and heard Jesus in the streets. However, to know that he was innocent ("righteous," RSV; "noble," MSG; "just," KJV) had to be revealed in her spirit. Some commentators attribute her dream to the devil, suggesting that Satan hoped to prevent Jesus' death and our redemption. However, I believe that only the Holy Spirit could have revealed to her that Jesus was innocent of any charges brought against him. I believe that God sent this dream to warn Pilate.

The question then became, would she keep the dream to herself or should she speak out? After all, women's voices were not valued or honored as men's were in that time and culture—especially not in a formal, legal setting such as the governor's court. But Pilate's wife, a woman of both courage and compassion, chose to exercise her voice against the odds.

She reached out to her husband and advised him that she had "suffered a great deal." The content of the dream was like nothing she had experienced before. It actually broke into her waking state of consciousness. We do not know what images passed before her mind's eye, but they frightened her and caused her anxiety. Immediately, she sent an alarming message to Pilate: "Have nothing to do with that innocent man."

Most dreams are forgotten. Some are mentionable, but few dreams impress us so greatly that we remember them for years. It is doubtful that any of us would send a message to a judge on the bench as a result of a dream. Pilate's wife, however, warned her husband before he delivered a verdict on Jesus' fate. Obviously the message did not stop him from allowing the Jewish leaders to crucify Jesus, but perhaps it was the echo of his wife's fear that had Pilate "washing his hands" of the whole affair.

Isn't it remarkable that during Jesus' long trial, no one pleaded for him but a woman?

Personal Story

I had been working for an industrial company for a few years. I started as a clerk and gradually earned my way to a manager's position. Shortly thereafter, the owners sold the company, and it became a subsidiary of a much larger organization. This provided the executives and employees an opportunity to have greater access to more diverse benefit plans and a variety of compensation opportunities, as well as training opportunities. Most employees were excited about the future of the company.

Several years later, the director of my department decided it was time to retire. Rather than selecting from within the company's many locations, his replacement was selected from one of the many subsidiaries. Although I was saddened by the departure of my immediate supervisor, I was excited and looking forward to new ideas and a different perspective and direction. This enthusiasm did not last long.

After the new director's arrival, I came to understand that he had not applied for this job. Under the reorganization, his existing duties were fading, so in order to keep employed, he accepted this position with limited training and experience. Within months, I was getting an uneasy feeling and having difficulty sleeping. I thought maybe I just needed to get over reporting to someone new. Then one night I had a dream.

The dream involved the entire office staff, as well as others I did not recognize. My new supervisor was telling everyone that he did not know where "it" was. I heard a voice say, "He is lying." Then I was viewing an unfamiliar car in a garage, which I recognized as the basement of the company's building. In the dream, my supervisor then said, "I was in a meeting." Again I heard a voice say, "He is lying." Then I was standing outside an apartment building. This street and building were not familiar to me either. I kept hearing the words, "He is lying."

The dream was so intense that it woke me up. For a few days, I pondered this dream. Weeks later, I happened to look out the window of my office into the company's parking lot, and there was the car. My supervisor was getting out of it.

One day a couple of weeks later, I was faced with acting on what I had seen and heard in my dream. A few gentlemen arrived at the company, asking to see my supervisor. The secretary brought them into the office area. When my supervisor entered the room, the men introduced themselves as police officers and asked to speak with him privately. My supervisor said that he did not have anything to say.

One of the police officers asked, "Where is the car?" I heard my supervisor say that he did not know. I immediately looked up at him. He said again that he did not know where the car was and that he had not seen it for months. The police officer asked those of us in the office area if we had seen this car. I spoke up and acknowledged that he had been driving the car a few days earlier. I suggested that they take a look in the basement of the building.

Upon doing so, the policemen located and retrieved the car. Apparently my supervisor had been trying to hide the vehicle from his soon-to-be ex-wife. The apartment building I had seen in my dream was the place where my supervisor met his girlfriend when he was supposed to be out of town attending a meeting.

I would like to say that my workplace was a wonderful environment to be in after that episode, but that would not be true. Within months I was laid off after ten years of employment.

All the same, acting on that dream was a life-changing experience for me. I had to learn to trust God in a different way. Although the Holy Spirit greatly impressed this dream on me, I needed courage to act on it. Unlike God, I could not see what would happen to me, the individual, or the company. However, through that experience, I learned that God can speak through dreams and visions. Although it may appear that acting on this dream may have cost me a job, it was one of the best choices I have ever made. And God was faithful to me. Within weeks of the layoff, I was working again, receiving a paycheck from my new employer, as well as severance payments from the previous employer.

Questions

1. Would you act on a prompting, dreams, or visions from God? Why or why not?
2. How has the story of Pilate's wife inspired you? Would you have the courage and faith to stand up for someone's innocence—especially in the face of much hostility and anger?
3. Do you think it would make a difference if you did stand up? Why or why not?

Thought for Your Day

"It is not who you are that holds you back, but it is who you think you are not."[2]

Closing Prayer

Heavenly Lord, thank you for the variety of ways you speak to us. Give us the courage and wisdom to communicate what you have given to us when needed or when we are called on. May we do this in love and service to you. Amen.

About the Writer

Jacqueline (Jackie) Brown is an ordained and licensed minister. She has a diploma in biblical theological studies and is currently obtaining her Master of Divinity, both from Palmer Theological Seminary. She is also a graduate of New Life Bible Institute Missionary Training School, where she received the Raymond Ayers Award and the Presidents' Special Recognition Award. Jackie serves on the board of directors for Christ Center for Dance.

NOTES

1. More detail can be found in the pseudepigraphical book *Acts of Pilate* (*Gospel of Nicodemus*), Bible Gateway, "All the Women of the Bible—Pilate's Wife," www.biblegateway.com/resources/all-women-bible/Pilate-8217-s-Wife.

2. Anonymous.

9

Mary and Martha

Do. Be. Do. Be. Do. Balance Is Important!

GABRIELLE HOWARD DAVIDSON

> *"Be still, and know that I am God!"*
> —PSALM 46:10

Hook Question

How do you know when you're doing too much?

Biblical Story

LUKE 10:38-42

Now as they went on their way, he entered a certain village, where a woman named Martha welcomed him into her home. She had a sister named Mary, who sat at the Lord's feet and listened to what he was saying. But Martha was distracted by her many tasks; so she came to him and asked, "Lord, do you not care that my sister has left me to do all the work by myself? Tell her then to help me." But the Lord answered her, "Martha, Martha, you are worried and distracted by many things; there is need of only one thing. Mary has chosen the better part, which will not be taken away from her."

Biblical Exposition

Sometimes in life we become so busy working for the kingdom that we don't take the time to replenish our own personal wellspring of God's love. Sometimes we can actually overdo it by thinking we are doing God's will, when indeed God's interest is for us to enter into God's rest. I believe this was the case with Mary and Martha when Jesus came to visit them. In the time of Christ and in long-standing Jewish tradition, in an honor-and-shame society, providing hospitality and service to others was required and considered honorable. So Martha was doing the honorable thing by serving her guests, and she was trying to get Jesus to shame her sister, Mary, into helping her. Jesus, in his usual reversal of paradigms, suggested that what Mary was doing—sitting at his feet in the posture of a student learning from the Master—was equally honorable. This was unusual because women were not expected (or allowed!) to study under rabbis.

Many times in the Bible, individuals and even whole nations are seen seeking God's will for their lives, and they do this by going to God in prayer and by fasting. In some cases they were told to continue in the path they had been considering, and sometimes they were told to be still and not move until God was with them.

The discipline of being still, of listening, of studying until God's Word and way are clear are the tasks of a disciple, a learner. How often do we, like the disciples, need to ask the Spirit to explain the lessons God is teaching because we do not understand them? In my own life, I have found that the more time I spend in prayer and study, the more I get out of the Scripture passages I am reading. This allows for the Holy Spirit to help me understand how a particular passage might apply to my daily living.

Personal Story

By 2012 I had spent seven and a half years caring for my mother who had Alzheimer's. I was married to my second husband, caring half-time for my two children from my first marriage, and going to school full-time. As I continued to develop my personal relationship with God through praying, I began to spend more and more time in morning devotion. At the same time, God slowly stripped away my responsibility as a wife, as a caregiver to my mother, and ultimately as custodial parent to my children. God also stripped me of all of the income that had been coming into the house. I was truly required to get to know God as my Jehovah Jireh—my provider.

First, my husband left in March; then in early June the hospice care agency recommended that my mother be released from rehab and be brought home to die. (After almost 7 years with Alzheimer's Disease, my mother had begun to deteriorate physically. She had been in and out of the hospital over the previous 6 months for urinary tract infections, had developed bed sores, had begun not eating, lost weight, and had to be fed via a tube.) While walking back into the classroom (I was enrolled in Masters of Divinity courses, studying to become a religious leader/pastor) after taking that call, I burst into tears. God told me at that point to "ask for help." I entered the room in tears, and my classmates surrounded me with prayer.

A few days after my mother passed away, my nephew called to say he had been shot and to ask if I would visit him in the hospital. When I visited him in the hospital, he asked if I would go home to get him a charger for his phone. As I jumped in my car to go home to get him a phone charger, the car would not start. At that time, I figured God wanted to tell me something else, so I spent some time with God in prayer in the car. It was at that time that God told me, "Know that you know that you know that I will provide for you." After spending about half an hour in the car, it simply started again when I tried it.

When I broke a bone in my leg in mid-August, I found out what Jehovah Jireh, "the Lord is my provider," truly means. I had to rely on my Christian friends to come and prepare meals for me, to pick me up and take me back and forth to school, and to go to the market for me. In addition, because all of my household income had gone away with my husband leaving and my mother passing away, I had to be fully reliant on the "manna" God was offering to me. I had to rely on God's supply for my financial needs, including trusting the Lord for my food. And when I was able to drive again, friends filled my gas tank. Instead of trading responsibilities for my daughters every two weeks, my children's father agreed to keep them on a full-time basis so that I could heal.

During this time I recognized that God was intending for me to spend more time in prayer and devotion and less time doing things for others. This was a time when people were pouring into me and doing for me. I was beginning to feel that "peace which surpasses all understanding" (Philippians 4:7) I had heard so much about. I felt as if I was entering into God's rest (Hebrews 3 and 4).

In the story of Mary and Martha, I see two sides of the same coin. I see my God showing us that we have both the ability to do things we believe are God's will and the ability to sit and be still with God. We are to value and enjoy that sitting time. God wants us to realize that our physical service is invaluable but that our stillness in prayer, love, and devotion is equally valuable.

Questions

1. Do you ever get caught up "doing" and forget just to "be"? Describe a time when your body responded to the amount of work or effort you were expending by forcing you to rest.

2. Consider a time when you felt you were pushing yourself too far. Did you slow down or did you continue to press through? What was the result?
3. What fail-safe methods have you put in place to help you to rest before you do too much?
4. When do you spend time alone with God? What kind of things do you do during these times?

Thought for Your Day

Balance is important. In what ways will I do God's will today, and in what ways will I just "be" in God's presence?

Closing Prayer

Dear Lord, help us to know when we are in need of private time alone with you. Please remind us that the time we spend devoted to studying your Word and worshipping you is equally as important as the time we spend doing for others in the world. Help us to remember to ask for replenishing of living water so that we may continue to pour ourselves into others in our daily walk. In Jesus' name, Amen.

About the Writer

Gabrielle Howard Davidson is a seminary student at Palmer Theological Seminary and a lifelong member of Zion Baptist Church of Philadelphia, Pennsylvania. She is a career counselor, small business consultant, and self-published author of *Career Management Track™ Workbook* for career transitioning and *Ready, Set, Goals! Motivational Implementation Planner*. She resides in Philadelphia with her two daughters.

Part 3

Women Who Led

10

Deborah

Arise, Arise!

STEFANIE WILSON

> "The peasantry prospered in Israel,
> they grew fat on plunder,
> because you arose, Deborah,
> arose as a mother in Israel."
> —JUDGES 5:7

Hook Question

When have you saved the day? What might have happened if you hadn't risen to the occasion?

Biblical Story

JUDGES 4:3-9, 12-14

Then the Israelites cried out to the LORD for help; for he had nine hundred chariots of iron, and had oppressed the Israelites cruelly twenty years. At that time Deborah, a prophetess, wife of Lappidoth, was judging Israel. She used to sit under the palm of Deborah between Ramah and Bethel in the hill country of Ephraim; and the Israelites came up to her for judgment. She sent and summoned Barak son of Abinoam from Kedesh in Naphtali, and said to him, "The LORD, the

God of Israel, commands you, 'Go, take position at Mount Tabor, bringing ten thousand from the tribe of Naphtali and the tribe of Zebulun. I will draw out Sisera, the general of Jabin's army, to meet you by the Wadi Kishon with his chariots and his troops; and I will give him into your hand.'" Barak said to her, "If you will go with me, I will go; but if you will not go with me, I will not go." And she said, "I will surely go with you; nevertheless, the road on which you are going will not lead to your glory, for the LORD will sell Sisera into the hand of a woman." Then Deborah got up and went with Barak to Kedesh. . . .

When Sisera was told that Barak son of Abinoam had gone up to Mount Tabor, Sisera called out all his chariots, nine hundred chariots of iron, and all the troops who were with him, from Harosheth-ha-goiim to the Wadi Kishon. Then Deborah said to Barak, "Up! For this is the day on which the LORD has given Sisera into your hand. The LORD is indeed going out before you." So Barak went down from Mount Tabor with ten thousand warriors following him.

Biblical Exposition

Israel had an ongoing pattern that is highlighted in the book of Judges. The Israelites sinned, God punished them, they cried out, and God sent them a deliverer. After a judge named Ehud died, Israel was once again in trouble—big trouble! They had been sold into the hands of King Jabin of Canaan, who had nine hundred chariots and used his wealth, military technology, and power to oppress the Israelites. This was a cruel endeavor that persisted for twenty years. As the people cried out, God sent a new judge, Deborah.

Deborah was quite an anomaly in that not only was she a female judge, but she was also recognized as a prophet and a "mother in Israel."

Deborah lived in a patriarchal system where men were dominant and women had extremely limited access to positions of power and influence. Yet Deborah found ways to differentiate herself from existing models of leadership. Unlike other judges who were known and chosen for their military prowess and charismatic leadership, Deborah actually *judged*. She sat among the people day in and day out and was available to them under her palm tree where she settled disputes. She used her God-given wisdom and leadership skills to bring peace and order to the community.

Being judge and prophet was no easy task. Deborah's self-confidence and assuredness were demonstrated, however, when Barak, the military leader, sought her presence on the battlefield. Although it may appear as though Barak was usurping her orders by demanding that she go with him on the battlefield, it would not have been unreasonable for a military leader to ask a prophet to accompany him. In essence, Barak was afraid that if he didn't have Deborah around, the victory may not be assured. Unfortunately, his dependence was mistakenly on her and not on the God she represented. One has to admire the fact that Deborah was not tempted to play the role of savior in this story. Although she agreed to go with Barak, she prophesied that the glory of victory would go to a woman, whom we eventually discover as the story unfolds with yet another twist, was not her.

Most of the leaders portrayed in the book of Judges were self-serving and unpredictable, and ruled according to their whims and personalities. As a prophet Deborah did not act on her own desires but sought God's will in decision making. Inspired by divine revelation, she unswervingly rallied the people to rise up and work toward freedom, encouraging them to trust God for their liberation and victory in battle. Without her willingness to depend on God and act on God's word, the Israelites would have remained under oppression.

Not only was Deborah a judge and prophet, but she was called "a mother in Israel." Prior to Deborah's rule, people lived in fear and oppression. Judges 5:6 says, "In the days of Shamgar son of Anath, in the days of Jael, caravans ceased and travelers kept to the byways." This meant that people had to stay off the roads while traveling for fear that they may be robbed or killed. This reign of terror stopped trade and greatly diminished the ability to provide for one's family. Every day life was strenuous and unsure. The Israelites' lives were slowly wasting away. Deborah, however, turned things around through her willingness to arise and embrace her God-given role.

Barak's song in Judges 5:7 says, "The peasantry prospered in Israel, they grew fat on plunder, because you arose, Deborah, arose as a mother in Israel." There is no way to be sure if Deborah was a biological or even adoptive mother to children of her own; however, it is clear that she was a spiritual mother. She counseled and directed the children of Israel; she nurtured them under the palm tree and sought to ensure their safety, security, and prosperity. She stayed with Barak, accompanying him when he was unwilling to go into battle without her. She walked with those she was leading. As Deborah arose as a maternal leader, prosperity and freedom returned to her people.

Personal Story

As I made my way through the viewing line at the funeral of a young man in his twenties who had died from a heroin overdose, I was devastated. This was the ninth funeral I had been to in five months. The string of deaths started with my precious brother-in-law who had passed away at the age of forty-three from a ten-month bout with melanoma. By the time I reached the casket of this young man, I was ready to quit ministry, crawl in a hole, and cry for a good while. As I approached the casket, his young wife threw herself into my arms and wailed. Then I encountered his mother, a friend and ministry partner of mine. She hugged me and looked into my eyes and said, "Remember, Stefanie, when you prayed with me to let him go like Moses' mother let him go? Because you ministered to me, I was able to let him go that night and give him to God. I never gave up, but I let him go."

Sometimes we all grow weary and want to give up, but if we did give up, others might not experience the healing, comfort, or liberation God has for them. Like Deborah, we must arise.

Arising is not always an easy thing, especially for women. Both women and men deal with the burdens of living everyday life, but for women, many hindrances emerge from living in a culture that sees women as inferior to men. Having been a part of churches that frowned on women in leadership, heralding it as unbiblical, I held Deborah close to my heart. When people said that "women shouldn't have authority over men," I would question myself and think I should give up dreaming of being a leader in the church. I feared that I was being "unbiblical." Then Deborah would come to my mind. You could say she was my only role model for women in leadership in the church. Her diversity of giftings and her self-assuredness in her leadership challenged me to trust and stand firm in God's calling so that I could have a life-giving impact on the lives of others.

I often wonder if, growing up, Deborah ever experienced a woman in power. I wonder what it was that gave her the strength to step forward into her divine calling. No doubt God called her, gifted her, and sustained her. As she began her journey into judgeship, perhaps she imparted her wisdom to neighbors and her own family and word spread of her anointing. In making herself available to others with diligence and steadfastness, she must have gained the trust and respect of those around her to the point that she became a natural choice for the judgeship.

As we seek to embody God's calling and gifting in our lives, we, like Deborah, can benefit in working incrementally and gaining the trust of those around us by being faithful in the little things. The only leadership offered to me in the church was over children's ministry unless I partnered with a man who assumed a position above me. For years I learned to minister and use my God-given gifts within these constraints. There were times this discouraged me, but year by year people began to trust my ministry and see God's anointing of leadership in my life. Through my obedience and God's intervention, I was provided with opportunities to lead, even in systems that normally denied women leadership.

A few years ago my husband and I planted a church and I was ordained as a founding pastor and elder. Ministry no doubt has been difficult and demanding. As a wife, mother, pastor, and full-time student, I have desired to quit many times. But then I have moments like I experienced at the funeral, when someone expresses how I have, through God's grace and power, helped them in their journey. If I had quit, I'm pretty sure God would have called someone else, but I would have missed out on the blessing of being a part of God's action in the world. My prayer is that each one of us would, like Deborah, despite the obstacles, arise and embrace with confidence and assurance the God-given gifts and call in our lives.

Questions

1. What are the gifts God has given you to use for kingdom work? What do you sense God is calling you to do with those gifts?
2. What has hindered you from following God's call and embracing God's gifting in your life?
3. In what areas have you been faithful to God's call and seen success?
4. Deborah managed to balance many different roles in her life. How are you managing the various roles you fulfill in your life? What can you do to maintain balance?
5. How has the story of Deborah inspired you?

Thought for Your Day

An African proverb says, "I am because you are." As we embrace who we are and operate in our God-given identity and calling, we enable others to also embrace who they are.

Closing Prayer

God, we thank you that you have gifted each one of us so that we can participate in your mission of setting captives free. Help us to embrace our calling despite the obstacles and to stand firm in who you created us to be. Amen.

About the Writer

Stefanie Wilson completed her Master of Divinity at Palmer Theological Seminary and is a founding pastor and elder of Bridgetown Fellowship Church in Coatesville, Pennsylvania. Stefanie also works part-time as a hospice chaplain. She has three children and has been married to her husband and co-pastor, Steve, for seventeen years.

11

Queen of Sheba
Truly Deserving of Blessings

KIMEISHA McLAREN

> *Behold, I found there a woman ruling over them;*
> *and she has been given [abundance] of all [good] things,*
> *and hers is a mighty throne.*
> —QUR'AN, SURAH 27: AN-NAML 23

Hook Question

Has anyone ever said that you don't deserve what has been given to you? How did that make you feel and what did you do about it?

Biblical Story

1 KINGS 10:1-10, 13
When the queen of Sheba heard of the fame of Solomon (fame due to the name of the LORD), she came to test him with hard questions. She came to Jerusalem with a very great retinue, with camels bearing spices, and very much gold, and precious stones; and when she came to Solomon, she told him all that was on her mind. Solomon answered all her questions; there was nothing hidden from the king that he could not explain to her. When the queen of Sheba had observed all the wisdom of

Solomon, the house that he had built, the food of his table, the seating of his officials, and the attendance of his servants, their clothing, his valets, and his burnt offerings that he offered at the house of the LORD, there was no more spirit in her.

So she said to the king, "The report was true that I heard in my own land of your accomplishments and of your wisdom, but I did not believe the reports until I came and my own eyes had seen it. Not even half had been told me; your wisdom and prosperity far surpass the report that I had heard. Happy are your wives! Happy are these your servants, who continually attend you and hear your wisdom! Blessed be the LORD your God, who has delighted in you and set you on the throne of Israel! Because the LORD loved Israel forever, he has made you king to execute justice and righteousness." Then she gave the king one hundred and twenty talents of gold, a great quantity of spices, and precious stones; never again did spices come in such quantity as that which the queen of Sheba gave to King Solomon. . . .

Meanwhile, King Solomon gave to the queen of Sheba every desire that she expressed, as well as what he gave her out of Solomon's royal bounty. Then she returned to her own land, with her servants.

QUR'ANIC STORY[1]
SURAH 27:23-33 TRANSLATED BY MUHAMMAD ASAD
In the following story, King Solomon is being told by his hoopoe bird about what he has found on his trip. The hoopoe is informing King Solomon that he has knowledge that King Solomon does not.

27:23 "Behold, I found there a woman ruling over them; and she has been given [abundance] of all [good] things, and hers is a mighty throne. 27:24 And I found her and her people adoring the sun instead of God; and Satan has made these doings of theirs seem goodly to them, and [thus] has barred them from the path [of God], so that they cannot find the right way: 27:25 [for they have come to believe] that they ought not to adore God—[although it is He] who brings forth all that is hidden in the heavens and on earth, and knows all that you would conceal as well as all that you bring into the open: 27:26 God, save whom there is no deity—the Sustainer, in awesome almightiness enthroned!"

27:27 Said [Solomon]: "We shall see whether thou hast told the truth or art one of the liars! 27:28 Go with this my letter and convey it to them; and thereafter withdraw from them and see what [answer] they return." 27:29 [When the queen had read Solomon's letter,] she said: "O you nobles! A truly distinguished letter has been conveyed unto me. 27:30 Behold, it is from Solomon, and it says, 'In the name of God, The Most Gracious, The Dispenser of Grace: 27:31 [God says:] Exalt not yourselves against Me, but come unto Me in willing surrender!'"

27:32 She added: "O you nobles! Give me your opinion on the problem with which I am now faced; I would never make a [weighty] decision unless you are present with me." 27:33 They answered: "We are endowed with power and with mighty prowess in war—but the command is thine; consider, then, what thou wouldst command."

Biblical Exposition

First Kings 3 tells the story of God appearing in a dream to King Solomon asking the king what God should give him. The king answered, "Give your servant therefore an understanding mind to govern your people, able to discern between good and evil; for who can govern this your great people?" (v. 9). Solomon became so known for his wisdom that 1 Kings 4:34 tells us that people from all over the earth heard of his wisdom. One of those people was the queen of Sheba.

We know very little about the queen of Sheba. Based on the biblical text, we know she was a woman with great wealth who was willing to speak her mind (1 Kings 10:2, 10), who came out of curiosity to see if what she had heard about the wisdom of King Solomon was really true (1 Kings 10:6). The queen of Sheba found that Solomon's wisdom surpassed what she had been told, and much has been made of verse 13: "Meanwhile King Solomon gave to the queen of Sheba every desire that she expressed."

The Qur'an paints a slightly different picture of the queen of Sheba, as it is she who has the mighty throne that is blessed by God (Allah), even if she does not understand it is God (Allah) who is blessing her. It is Solomon who wants to find out about the queen and sends a request for her to come to him and surrender. As the story continues in the Qur'an, they spar back and forth until the queen recognizes it is God (Allah), the Lord of the Worlds, who has blessed them both.

Personal Story

I chose to use the Qur'an version of the queen of Sheba story because it gives more insight into who she was as a ruler. The Qur'an touches on the vastness of her kingdom, and it shows that she possessed wisdom, as well. The biblical story does not give us the details about the queen that we encounter in the Qur'an. The queen did not come to seek out Solomon's knowledge; she came to verify it because she too possessed wisdom and knowledge.

After reading the story of the queen of Sheba, I reflected on my upbringing in Kingston, Jamaica; my family was a part of the working poor. I had two school uniforms and three pairs of school socks that I had to wash each day when I returned home from school in order to have them to wear the next day. My family was mostly Rastafarian and Seventh-day Adventist.

My upbringing was very humble. I am by no means rich even today. However, God has allowed me to be the first in my family to be college-educated, the first to enter the military, and the first to own a home (the bank and I currently own the home).

I have not forgotten my humble beginnings; I use them to ground me. However, I wonder if the queen of Sheba concerned herself with what others may have said about the vastness of her "queendom," the might of her army, or the power of her throne.

I wonder about this because I have been told that my faith/ beliefs are not correct. I don't see myself as only a Rastafarian, nor a Seventh-day Adventist, or a Christian. My faith and beliefs are now built on all of the faith experiences that I've had. Family members and associates have accused me of behaving like "I'm all that." They would begin to list some of my blessings and say that I don't deserve them. This used to bother me. I would withdraw and analyze myself and question what was said to me.

I do not possess what the queen possessed; however, I know that what I have been given are blessings from God. I do not compare my blessings to those of others, nor do I concern myself with how God chooses to bless God's creation. I know the queen of Sheba did not serve the God of Solomon; however, that does not mean that God is not capable of blessing her. Nebuchadnezzar was a Babylonian whom God punished for giving himself credit for what God had blessed him with. Babylonians were not known for believing in the God of Moses.

What I have come to understand is that my blessings are from my Creator as were the blessings of Sheba. All that was under her rule was from her Creator, and all that I have been given and will be given comes from my Creator. Solomon's encounter and letter to Sheba was orchestrated and designed by God. God does not make mistakes; God creates opportunities, and they are there for those who choose to see them as such.

God's bounty is limitless. I will be grateful for all God has given me, be it small or great, because it all comes from God. I no longer think about whether I am deserving of my blessings. No one chooses better than God. I know that once I am blessed, I should seek ways to be a blessing to someone else.

Questions

1. Does anyone possess a better plan for your life than God, and if so, how does that plan stand up against God's plan?
2. How can we better respond to individuals who tell us we are unworthy of our blessings?
3. Do you trust the choices God has made for your life so far? If so, why?
4. How can you use your blessings from God to help bless someone else?

Thought for Your Day

Accept your blessings with thanksgiving, knowing that God is the best of choosers and planners.

Closing Prayer

Oh Allah, I am thankful that you have chosen to bless me. Not because of anything that I have done, but because of who you are. Let me be always reminded to give you the honor, glory, and praise for being my sustainer, protector, and provider. Allow me to use my blessing(s) to be a blessing. Amen.

Allah defined: The Supreme Being; God. According to Islamreligion.com, Allah is the Arabic word for God. "Al," the definite article, means "the," and "lah" means God. As believers we must be reminded that the earth is filled with many different languages and dialects. This understanding should allow us to accept the many different names of God. Allah is not a "Muslim God." Allah is God's name in Arabic, the God of Abraham, Noah, Moses, and Jesus, peace be upon them all.

About the Writer

Kimeisha McLaren is completing her Master of Theological Studies with a concentration in biblical studies at Palmer Theological Seminary. She is of the Islamic faith and came to Palmer to study the Christian Bible. Kimeisha is a member at Quba Masjid in Philadelphia.

NOTES

1. Muhammad Asad, *The Message of The Qur'an* (Gibraltar: Dar-Al-Andalus, 1980), 578–82.

12

Huldah

Can a Woman Teach a Man?

DEBORAH SPINK WINTERS

> The King said, "Go, inquire of the LORD for me,
> for the people, and for all Judah, concerning the words
> of this book that has been found. . . . So the priest
> Hilkiah, Ahikam, Achbor, Shaphan, and Asaiah
> went to the prophetess Huldah."
> —2 KINGS 22:13-14

Hook Question

When have you wanted to do something, maybe even felt called to do it, only to have someone else tell you that because of your age, abilities, gender, ethnicity, religion, etc., you could not? How did you respond?

Biblical Story

2 KINGS 22:8-20

The high priest Hilkiah said to Shaphan the secretary, "I have found the book of the law in the house of the LORD." When Hilkiah gave the book to Shaphan, he read it. Then Shaphan the secretary came to the king, and reported to the king, "Your servants have emptied out the money that was found in the house, and have delivered it into the hand of the workers who have oversight of the house of the LORD." Shaphan the secretary informed the king, "The priest Hilkiah has given me a book." Shaphan then read it aloud to the king.

When the king heard the words of the book of the law, he tore his clothes. Then the king commanded the priest Hilkiah, Ahikam son of Shaphan, Achbor son of Micaiah, Shaphan the secretary, and the king's servant Asaiah, saying, "Go, inquire of the LORD for me, for the people, and for all Judah, concerning the words of this book that has been found; for great is the wrath of the LORD that is kindled against us, because our ancestors did not obey the words of this book, to do according to all that is written concerning us."

So the priest Hilkiah, Ahikam, Achbor, Shaphan, and Asaiah went to the prophetess Huldah the wife of Shallum son of Tikvah, son of Harhas, keeper of the wardrobe; she resided in Jerusalem in the Second Quarter, where they consulted her.

Biblical Exposition

King Josiah is one of the few kings of whom the narrator comments, "He did what was right in the sight of the LORD and walked in all the way of his father David; he did not turn aside to the right or to the left" (2 Kings 22:2). When King Josiah was twenty-six years old and in the eighteenth year of his reign, he decided it was time to repair the house of the Lord, the temple. While the temple was being repaired, the high priest Hilkiah found the book of the law.

There is some question as to whether the book of the law was really "found" (that is, that it had been lost and was suddenly found or had been found when no one even knew it existed), or whether it had been strategically placed in the temple to be found, possibly by survivors of the northern kingdom of Israel so their sacred texts would not be lost.

When the high priest told the king about the book of the law he had found, the king tore his clothes, which in the culture of that day meant there was something terribly wrong that needed to be fixed if at all possible. The king commanded the high priest and others to inquire of the Lord concerning the book of the law that had been found so that they would be sure to follow it.

It is interesting that the high priest did not go to confer with the prophets Jeremiah or Zephaniah, both of whom were probably ministering at that time, but instead took the book to a woman, to the prophet Huldah, the wife of a temple official.

Was the fact that the high priest took the book to the wife of a temple official more proof that the book had been strategically placed in the temple? Or should we be more amazed that in a time and culture that did not recognize women as first-class citizens, a woman was given the authority to interpret the book of the law, believed to be a part of the book of Deuteronomy?

Just when we think women have no say or authority in the biblical text, suddenly we read about the prophet Deborah or the prophet Huldah, both recognized for the gifts God had given them. It is these women of the Bible God used to change my life.

Personal Story

I grew up in a church where the pastor was male and all the pastors before him were male. I read Scriptures telling me that a woman was not to teach a man (1 Timothy 2:12) and that women were to keep silent in church (1 Corinthians 14:34). One day while studying the Scriptures, I was surprised when I came across the story of Huldah, a woman in the Old Testament who lived during the reign of King Josiah.

At a time when King Josiah was directing his men to help renovate the temple, they came across a book of the law, part of the Torah (part of our Bible today). To make sure it was authentic, they took it to a prophet to authenticate it and to teach the king and the priests and the officials what it meant.

That prophet was a woman! She not only taught the men what the biblical text said but also interpreted what it meant for them. How could this be?

Why in the Old Testament was a woman allowed to teach men and interpret the biblical text to them, but by the time of the New Testament letters, women were prohibited from doing those same things? What happened? Does that mean women being asked to teach men and then not teach men was only for a specific time? And what does that mean for women today?

As I began to study the biblical text, I found out that Huldah was not the only woman considered a prophet, someone who spoke for God. Moses' sister Miriam was a prophet (Exodus 15:20). Deborah was a prophet and a judge (Judges 4:4)! Philip the evangelist had four daughters with the gift of prophecy (Acts 21:8-9), Phoebe is called a deacon (Romans 16:1-2), and Junia was considered an apostle (Romans 16:7)!

The more I studied the biblical text, the more excited I became. I was beginning to feel the call of God on my life but still struggled with the tension of what to do with these biblical texts in 1 Timothy and 1 Corinthians that clearly taught that women in the church should be silent and should not teach men. At the same time, however, I recognized that the biblical text uplifted women like Miriam, Deborah, Phoebe, and Junia, who did not keep silent but rather used the gifts God had given them to teach both men and women.

When I finally made the decision to go to seminary, most of my friends told me it was about time, for they had recognized the gifts of teaching and preaching God had given me long before I did. In seminary I began to learn that every part of the Bible was written at a specific time in history to a specific audience. One of our jobs as interpreters of the biblical text is to understand the context that each of the biblical books was written in, what issues it addressed for its specific audience, and what it means for us today.

I learned that 1 Timothy and 1 Corinthians deal with specific situations in particular historical and cultural contexts. The text in 1 Timothy addresses the issue of uneducated women teaching and possibly abusing their authority. First Corinthians addresses the problem of unlearned women interrupting and slowing down the congregational teaching. In both cases, the women needed to be educated in the biblical text before they began to teach.[1]

As I placed those texts within the whole biblical framework, I learned that Joel 2:28-32 tells of the day when sons *and* daughters will prophesy, of Jesus' revolutionary way of treating women in the context of his day, and of Paul's declaration that in Christ there is no longer male nor female (Galatians 3:28), for all are gifted and are to develop their gifts and use them for the glory of God.

As I have grown in my ministry, I have learned that there are people who are not ready to hear God's message through me because I am a woman or because of my race or because of my age or because of the way I speak. As I brush the dust of that place off my feet and prepare to move on, I pray that maybe a little dirt has been loosened or perhaps a seed has been planted that I know nothing about. I pray that God will send the next person to do the planting or watering or to have the joy of harvesting. As for me, I keep studying and asking the Holy Spirit for guidance to help me use the gift of teaching and preaching to the glory of God.

Questions

1. In what situations (if any) might it be better for either a man or a woman to teach the biblical text?
2. What does it mean to you that there is no longer male and female, for we are all one in Christ?
3. What is it you feel God calling you to do that you do not feel ready for? Why?

4. What gift do you know God has given you that you need to develop more? What are the various ways you can develop your gift?

Thought for Your Day

"In Christ's family there can be no division into Jew and non-Jew, slave and free, male and female. Among us you are all equal." (Galatians 3:28, MSG)

Closing Prayer

Dear God, thank you for the gifts you have given us, male and female alike. Help us to trust you as we develop and use those gifts to glorify you. Amen.

About the Writer

Rev. Dr. Deborah Spink Winters is an affiliate professor of Old Testament at Palmer Theological Seminary at Eastern University, on the faculty of www.coaching4clergy.com, co-founder of www.GodsPreciousChildren.com, a Professional Certified Coach with the International Coaching Foundation, founder of www.debwinterscoaching.com, and an ordained pastor in the United Church of Christ.

NOTES

1. For a full discussion on this material, see Craig S. Keener, *Paul, Women, and Wives: Marriage and Women's Ministry in the Letters of Paul* (Henrickson Publishers, Inc., 1992), 70–132.

13

Vashti

You're Not the Boss of Me!

MONICA WASHINGTON

> [The king] sent letters to all the royal provinces,
> to every province in its own script and to every people
> in its own language, declaring that every man should
> be master in his own house.
> —ESTHER 1:22

Hook Question

How can we learn to love in a way that frees us and not enslaves us?

Biblical Story

ESTHER 1:1-12

This happened in the days of Ahasuerus, the same Ahasuerus who ruled over one hundred twenty-seven provinces from India to Ethiopia. In those days when King Ahasuerus sat on his royal throne in the citadel of Susa, in the third year of his reign, he gave a banquet for all his officials and ministers. The army of Persia and Media and the nobles and governors of the provinces were present, while he displayed the great wealth of his kingdom and the splendor and pomp of his majesty for many days, one hundred eighty days in all.

When these days were completed, the king gave for all the people present in the citadel of Susa, both great and small, a banquet lasting for seven days, in the court of the garden of the king's palace. There were white cotton curtains and blue hangings tied with cords of fine linen and purple to silver rings and marble pillars. There were couches of gold and silver on a mosaic pavement of porphyry, marble, mother-of-pearl, and colored stones. Drinks were served in golden goblets, goblets of different kinds, and the royal wine was lavished according to the bounty of the king. Drinking was by flagons, without restraint; for the king had given orders to all the officials of his palace to do as each one desired. Furthermore, Queen Vashti gave a banquet for the women in the palace of King Ahasuerus.

On the seventh day, when the king was merry with wine, he commanded Mehuman, Biztha, Harbona, Bigtha and Abagtha, Zethar and Carkas, the seven eunuchs who attended him, to bring Queen Vashti before the king, wearing the royal crown, in order to show the peoples and the officials her beauty; for she was fair to behold. But Queen Vashti refused to come at the king's command conveyed by the eunuchs. At this the king was enraged, and his anger burned within him.

Biblical Exposition

The Persians were known for their parties. King Ahasuerus partied for 180 days—first hosting a gala for his officials and then for the people living within the walls of Susa. And while the king was throwing his parties, Queen Vashti decided to throw a party of her own for all the women in the palace.

It was in the midst of these parties that the king, "merry with wine," decided to show off his queen as one would show off a trophy. He ordered Queen Vashti to come wearing the royal crown so that he could parade her beauty in front of everyone.

Questions have been raised about this verse: did the king want Vashti to come and make sure she was wearing her crown, or did he want her to come wearing *only* her crown? What would you do if your spouse, in a drunken stupor, commanded you to parade in front of a bunch of drunken friends wearing only a crown on your head?

At great personal risk—she could have been sentenced to death—Queen Vashti took a stand for who she was and for her own sense of worth and said no. Because of her stand, she lost the position of queen, but as best we can tell from the biblical text, she did not lose her life—or her own self-respect.

Personal Story

When I was sixteen, I fell in love with someone who I thought had it all together. He came from a close family and appeared to be a decent guy. I was young and, as I reflect on this now, I probably had low self-esteem. I didn't see myself as beautiful because I had been a tomboy most of my childhood. I thought I would never find someone of his caliber who would want me, especially an unattractive me.

I held on to him very tightly in my heart. From the beginning he never treated me right, but something within me would not let him go. He came and went whenever he felt like it. He dated me and other girls at the same time. He spoke negatively about me all the time to my family, to his family, in front of my face, and behind my back. He had no respect for me, and I allowed it.

Years went by. We had children together, purchased property together, and traveled together. Everything we did was what he wanted to do and never what I suggested. We only did things with his family and went places with his family, and as a result I became estranged from my family.

The longer I stayed with him, the more the possibility of who I could be was wrapped up in him. I never had the chance to see what my identity would be because we began dating as young teenagers—at a time when we began to establish who we were as individuals.

I stayed with him for twenty years, being verbally, physically, and mentally abused and financially destroyed. An act of God pulled me out of that relationship with this man. I believed in God and I was raised up in the church, so I knew who God was. In my moments of sadness, I would read the Bible, and toward the end of the relationship, I found myself spending more time with God. I believe that God was weaning me from this relationship because it had finally reached its demise. Enduring that kind of heartache was very painful for me as a person, as a mother, and as a woman. But I got through it with God's help.

Vashti represented what I wasn't. She knew her worth, and she didn't compromise it for anybody else, not even her husband, the man she loved. She was willing to walk away from him rather than have him exploit her by showing her off like she was a dancer in a strip club to all his drunken friends.

Vashti did what I wish I had done long before our relationship went into twenty years of turmoil. Vashti was a strong woman who knew her worth and demanded respect for herself. Although she was banished from the kingdom, she still walked away with dignity and respect.

Questions

1. How could Vashti's situation possibly have had a different ending?
2. How do you believe Jesus would have responded to the Vashti story and the personal story?
3. How do we maintain a healthy sense of self while being joined together as one with our mates?

4. What stands do you feel you need to take in your life, in your marriage, in your church, and in your faith?

Thought for Your Day

"Husbands love your wives, just as Christ loved the church and gave himself up for her" (Ephesians 5:25).

Closing Prayer

Eternal God, we thank you for the love you have shown us and given to us. We pray that you instill that same love in us that we may practice it in our daily lives and within our relationships with others. May the world give you all the glory when they see you working in our lives. Amen.

About the Writer

Monica Washington is a student at Palmer Theological Seminary and an ordained pastor at Mercy Seat Cathedral Church in Philadelphia. Monica is also founder of When God Heals a Woman, a nonprofit organization created to address the disparities of women everywhere through education, conferences, public resources, and awareness.

14

Esther

Women of Faith Are Women of Strength and Endless Power

SHANI AKILAH JOHNSON

> "For if you keep silent at such a time as this, relief
> and deliverance will rise for the Jews from another
> quarter, but you and your father's family will perish.
> Who knows? Perhaps you have come to royal dignity
> for just such a time as this."
> —ESTHER 4:14

Hook Question

How do you rate your self-esteem and self-confidence?

Biblical Story

ESTHER 4:1-17

When Mordecai learned all that had been done, Mordecai tore his clothes and put on sackcloth and ashes, and went through the city, wailing with a loud and bitter cry; he went up to the entrance of the king's gate, for no one might enter the king's gate clothed with sackcloth. In every province, wherever the king's command and his decree came, there was great mourning among the Jews, with fasting and weeping and lamenting, and most of them lay in sackcloth and ashes.

When Esther's maids and her eunuchs came and told her, the queen was deeply distressed; she sent garments to clothe Mordecai, so that he might take off his sackcloth; but he would not accept them. Then Esther called for Hathach, one of the king's eunuchs, who had been appointed to attend her, and ordered him to go to Mordecai to learn what was happening and why. Hathach went out to Mordecai in the open square of the city in front of the king's gate, and Mordecai told him all that had happened to him, and the exact sum of money that Haman had promised to pay into the king's treasuries for the destruction of the Jews. Mordecai also gave him a copy of the written decree issued in Susa for their destruction, that he might show it to Esther, explain it to her, and charge her to go to the king to make supplication to him and entreat him for her people.

Hathach went and told Esther what Mordecai had said. Then Esther spoke to Hathach and gave him a message for Mordecai, saying, "All the king's servants and the people of the king's provinces know that if any man or woman goes to the king inside the inner court without being called, there is but one law—all alike are to be put to death. Only if the king holds out the golden scepter to someone, may that person live. I myself have not been called to come in to the king for thirty days." When they told Mordecai what Esther had said, Mordecai told them to reply to Esther, "Do not think that in the king's palace you will escape any more than all the other Jews. For if you keep silence at such a time as this, relief and deliverance will rise for the Jews from another quarter, but you and your father's family will perish. Who knows? Perhaps you have come to royal dignity for just such a time as this." Then Esther said in reply to Mordecai, "Go, gather all the Jews to be found in Susa, and hold a fast on my behalf, and neither eat nor drink for three days, night or day. I and my maids will also fast as you do. After that I will go to the king, though it is against the law; and if I perish, I perish." Mordecai then went away and did everything as Esther had ordered him.

Biblical Exposition

If anybody knew about the blistering crawl through the tunnels of opposition, it was Queen Esther. When Esther's parents died, her relative Mordecai adopted her. The young woman had more obstacles ahead of her. Undoubtedly, Esther's life gained much stress in a very short time when she was chosen to be the next queen in a beauty pageant hosted by Ahasuerus, the fourth king of the Achaemenid Empire. From being an orphan to being in a very scary leadership position as queen, Esther had to have known all about the paralyzing effects of trepidation.

Mordecai sent word to Esther that she must go to the king and stop the assassination order put out on her people. Esther was afraid because she knew that anyone who faced the king without being summoned accepted the possibility of death. Mordecai saw things through a different lens and told Esther, "Do not think that in the king's palace you will escape any more than all the other Jews. For if you keep silence at such a time as this, relief and deliverance will rise for the Jews from another quarter, but you and your father's family will perish. Who knows? Perhaps you have come to royal dignity for just such a time as this" (4:13-14).

With great courage, Esther agreed to go to the king but told Mordecai to request all the Jews to fast for three days and repent for their own sins while praying for the decree against them to be reversed. It was because of her courage that the Jewish people in Persia were allowed to defend and save themselves. Queen Esther is an example of faith, willpower, wisdom, courage, strength, tenacity, elegance, and a recipe for powerful leadership that illustrates even today what a remarkable woman of the faith looks like.

Personal Story

I remember the first time I heard one of my male church leaders say that a woman is meant for the kitchen and bedroom. The same leader told me I was completely in denial of my position as a woman. He added, "You are thinking too highly of yourself. Y'all are always forcing yourselves into leadership—but God called the man to lead." I almost raised my voice and pointed my finger, but I decided to respond calmly, "Well, just wait and see. Trust me, while I am on earth, I will show you a woman who is called to lead." I walked away (of course elegantly and with a little more pep than usual).

When this male church leader shared his views on a woman's place in the world, I was affected—but only for a moment. Naturally, his searing views disturbed me, but I rejected them. I grew up in a time when women occupied all kinds of roles—as construction workers, athletes (including football players), mayors of cities, business owners, and many more. I have learned to soak in the greatness of influential women who demonstrate the powerful push that mirrors our "I can do all things through Christ" disposition.

Today I am living in a growing arena of female world leaders like Queen Elizabeth, Hillary Clinton, Oprah Winfrey, and Michelle Obama, who drape a global sisterhood with security and hope for our acceptance on a diverse stage of leadership.

When I think of strong women in the Bible, reflecting on Esther is inevitable. Like Esther, many of our world leaders have overcome great adversity and have landed on powerful platforms of social change. Esther is celebrated for risking her life to serve God and to save her people.

Undeniably, there is still a dark scrim over *our* leadership capabilities, as many still see women as sex objects and domestic agents. Even as we increase in number as ministers of the gospel, high-powered corporate executives, world leaders, and robust leaders within our local communities, many refuse to accept us as legitimate and equipped kingdom builders. Indeed, being a female minister comes with some attack against my self-esteem. Since seminary, I have heard all kind of things! I have been told my limitations as a pastoral leader, and most injurious, I have been treated like I am incompetent. Women have always dealt with the sting of low self-esteem, which is compounded as our abilities are denounced. This may never end, so we must remind ourselves never to listen to such foolishness.

Well, thank God Esther operated in a divine confidence and esteem that allowed her to protect her people and illuminated her outstanding characteristics as queen even more. I am choosing to do the same each day I live! I will land in some uncomfortable places, but I will move as Esther did, and simply lean on our God for divine power. Let us operate in this same confidence, no matter what.

Questions

1. What issues are you holding on to that are affecting your self-image and self-confidence in regard to leadership?
2. What women can you turn to for a powerful example of pushing and pressing in the faith?
3. What are your strong areas in leadership? How can you use your weak areas for further personal enhancement?
4. How does Esther speak to your self-esteem, personal image, and self-confidence?

Thought for Your Day

Our self-esteem must be ignited by our desire to be faithful to our awesome God. If we lean not on our own understanding, we will sparkle with divine purpose. To be called by God is to be certain of the amazing journey!

Closing Prayer

Gracious God, help us to see ourselves through your lenses. Let us hold on to your unconditional love as we surrender to the works you have assigned to us since the day of our conception. Amen.

About the Writer

Shani Akilah Johnson graduated from Palmer Theological Seminary in May 2014 with a Master of Divinity. A minister, singer, and writer from Philadelphia, Shani plans on traveling and merging her creative talents with her desire to preach and teach the gospel of Jesus Christ.

Part 4

Women Who Found Their Voice

15

Hannah

Society Should Not Define Your Life!

AGNES E. LAMIN

> *"Do not regard your servant as a worthless woman,
> for I have been speaking out of my great anxiety and
> vexation all this time."*
> —1 SAMUEL 1:16

Hook Question

How can people survive in a society where certain things are expected of them and they do not have the sole control of acquiring them?

Biblical Story

1 SAMUEL 1:1-11

There was a certain man of Ramathaim, a Zuphite from the hill country of Ephraim, whose name was Elkanah son of Jeroham son of Elihu son of Tohu son of Zuph, an Ephraimite. He had two wives; the name of the one was Hannah, and the name of the other Peninnah. Peninnah had children, but Hannah had no children.

Now this man used to go up year by year from his town to worship and to sacrifice to the LORD of hosts at Shiloh, where the two sons of Eli, Hophni and Phinehas, were priests of the LORD. On the day when Elkanah sacrificed, he would give portions to his wife Peninnah and to all her sons and daughters; but to Hannah he gave a double portion, because he loved her, though the LORD had closed her womb. Her rival used to provoke her severely, to irritate her, because the LORD had closed her womb. So it went on year by year; as often as she went up to the house of the LORD, she used to provoke her. Therefore Hannah wept and would not eat. Her husband Elkanah said to her, "Hannah, why do you weep? Why do you not eat? Why is your heart sad? Am I not more to you than ten sons?"

After they had eaten and drunk at Shiloh, Hannah rose and presented herself before the LORD. Now Eli the priest was sitting on the seat beside the doorpost of the temple of the LORD. She was deeply distressed and prayed to the LORD, and wept bitterly. She made this vow: "O LORD of hosts, if only you will look on the misery of your servant, and remember me, and not forget your servant, but will give to your servant a male child, then I will set him before you as a nazirite until the day of his death. He shall drink neither wine nor intoxicants, and no razor shall touch his head."

Biblical Exposition

Hannah lived at a time when the rule of the judges was coming to an end and the monarchical period of Israel was soon to begin. For a woman to be considered blessed by God in this time period, she had to be able to bear her husband children, preferably sons. Childless women were considered cursed by God and were looked down on by everyone in the community. If the primary wife was considered barren, the husband may have been pressured by the community to take a second wife in order to have children.

This may have been the exact situation Hannah found herself in. She was childless, and her beloved husband, Elkanah, took a second wife, Peninnah, who was able to bear him children so his name would live on and he would be considered blessed by God. Hannah would have been scorned by her entire community and especially by the second wife.

Hannah turned to the only one able to answer her prayer: God. It is interesting in this time frame that the desire to have a child may also be wrapped up in the desire to be accepted by the surrounding community. Did Hannah's vow show her deep desire to be a mother whatever the cost? Or did it show her gratitude to God that she would now be considered blessed and in that gratitude was willing to give the child back to God? Or did it show her desire to have a male child who would reestablish her acceptability in her community, even though she would not be the one raising her own child? Or was it perhaps a combination of them all? The story doesn't really tell us. What do you think?

Personal Story

Hannah's story has been a source of encouragement to me throughout my period of childlessness. My country of origin, Sierra Leone, a primarily Muslim country, is dominated by Islamic norms. Getting married and having children are expected of young women; for a woman to be unmarried at age twenty-one is considered shameful. As is common in Islam, polygamy is practiced in my country. A man is allowed to marry as many as four wives, although this does not mean he can take care of them all. He can live with all of his wives in one house, along with their children, in-laws, and other extended family members.

These wives find themselves in a competitive situation as they strive to win the heart of the husband. One of the means of getting into the man's heart is by taking care of his needs, such as washing his clothes, cooking the best food that he sometimes does not provide, cleaning his bedroom, since he sleeps in his own room, and producing (preferably) male children.

A wife needs to have children of her own to avoid being accused of being cursed. A child is a source of her strength. She needs children—preferably sons—to help her fetch wood, till the garden, carry water, and fight for her when the need arises.

Sadly, the church in my country also supports this idea of childbearing as a must. It is difficult to associate with those who are celebrating their children's successes when you have no children. You cannot bring up another's child and not expect society to remind you that you have none of your own. This is very hard, as you will have to live with it for the rest of your life.

When I decided to answer the call to serve the Lord and go to seminary, my family was quick to assume that this would be the end of society's expectation of me getting married and having children of my own. Women in my culture are expected to take care of their homes. Upon hearing my decision to live for and serve the Lord, my family called a meeting to try to persuade me not to take that route. But my mind was already made up, and nothing was going to stop me.

I have three sisters and two brothers, and subsequently my three sisters got married within two years, and they all have children of their own. They all gave birth last October, the same month as my mom's birthday. This has caused a whole lot of gossiping about me not being able to meet society's expectation; therefore I am considered a failure in life.

As in the case of Hannah, I have prayed and cried and gone for days without food, asking God to send me a husband so that I can have children. What has made matters worse is that having children out of wedlock is now both acceptable and celebrated. This has made it very difficult for me because my devotion to God will not allow me to have children outside of wedlock. My family and community do not understand this because they believe success in life depends on getting married or having children.

At times I used to look at myself as society has defined me: miserable. I would go for days without food, crying and praying and sometimes questioning God about why my prayers were going unanswered. I would complain and feel sorry for myself as though my life depended on having a husband and children. I had almost given up on life when I decided some time ago that I was going to quit ministry.

God began to answer my prayers in unexpected ways. One day I was preaching and touched on the subject of abortion. A woman in the congregation happened to be contemplating having one done. The Holy Spirit moved her to come talk to me after service. I decided to take care of her through her pregnancy until she gave birth. The woman named the baby after me and said the infant was mine.

Another woman who was helping me with my house chores also happened to become pregnant, and her husband denied the pregnancy. She came and told me about it and wanted to abort the baby since she had three already. I persuaded her not to do it and decided to support her as well. Upon delivery, she also named the baby after me. Before the woman left to stay with another man, she brought the child to me and asked me to take care of her for the rest of my life and said that she is my child. The woman passed away two years later. The child is presently living with my mom. Even though I took that child to church and dedicated her as my child, people still consider me as being childless.

One of my sisters who gave birth in October decided to name her child after me and called me on the phone and said, "This child belongs to you, and I'm only taking care of her until you return." As with Hannah, God had answered my prayers in another form. But because in my society you must be a biological mother, they do not regard that as a prayer being answered.

Hannah's response to Penninah's provocation and to her own barrenness provides a model for all of us and particularly for women in cultures where polygamy is practiced and a first wife may have to learn how to handle a second or third woman in her husband's life. Hannah could have responded to Penninah's provocation by simply continuing to fight with her, or she could have turned on her husband like Rachel did when she told Jacob, "Give me children, or I shall die!" (Genesis 30:1) and then insisted that he take her maidservant. She could have turned to witchcraft, either as a way to have children herself or to harm or kill Penninah's children, or she could have stopped loving and serving the Lord because her prayers had not been answered. But she did none of these things. Instead, she prayed fervently to the Lord. In her prayer she did not curse the day she was born or her wedding day. She did not ask the Lord to avenge her or vindicate her.

Hannah's story is one that also taught me to go to the Lord with every need and believe and trust that God can do all things. Even when the answer is not what I would like, I will keep on trusting and embracing what God has given me. Hannah also demonstrated that God owns all that we ever have when she gave her son back to God.

Questions

1. How do you handle situations that bring shame and pain because of what society has constructed?
2. What can you do to reflect Christ in the midst of your vulnerability?
3. How do you handle situations when you are being tried and tested in ministry?
4. How has the story of Hannah had an impact on your life or ministry?

Thought for Your Day

When we become desperate, we should turn to God and nowhere else, believing and trusting that God can do the impossible.

Closing Prayer

Eternal God in heaven, thank you for showing us that you are a God of diversity, not only in our gender, color, race, or origin, but also in our stories. Help us to understand our uniqueness in your plan and purpose for our existence. In Jesus' name we pray. Amen!

About the Writer

Agnes E. Lamin is an international student from Sierra Leone, West Africa, at Palmer Theological Seminary. She is ordained into full gospel ministry by the Baptist Convention of Sierra Leone. She is also the founder of Women at Risk–Sierra Leone, an organization that seeks to help women who are actively involved in prostitution become self-reliant and regain their self-worth through counseling, training, and advocacy.

16

Mother of James and John
No Foolish Questions

ELLA M. PARKS

> "Ask, and it will be given you; search, and you will
> find; knock, and the door will be opened for you.
> For everyone who asks receives, and everyone
> who searches finds, and for everyone who knocks,
> the door will be opened."
> —MATTHEW 7:7-8

Hook Question

Can we ask God for anything even if our motive is self-centered?

Biblical Story

MATTHEW 20:20-22

Then the mother of the sons of Zebedee came to him with her sons, and kneeling before him, she asked a favor of him. And he said to her, "What do you want?" She said to him, "Declare that these two sons of mine will sit, one at your right hand and one at your left, in your kingdom." But Jesus answered, "You do not know what you are asking. Are you able to drink the cup that I am about to drink?" They said to him, "We are able."

Biblical Exposition

The mother of James and John, also known as the sons of Zebedee, is one of the unnamed women of the Bible. She appears again in Matthew 27:56 as one of the woman who witnessed Jesus' death on the cross: "Among them were Mary Magdalene, and Mary the mother of James and Joseph, and the mother of the sons of Zebedee." Mark 15:40 also lists three women who were at the cross: "There were also women looking on from a distance; among them were Mary Magdalene, and Mary the mother of James the younger and of Joses, and Salome." Because Mark names the third woman as "Salome," some biblical scholars have speculated about whether Salome is the name of the mother of James and John, the sons of Zebedee. No one knows for sure.

In Mark 10:35-45 the sons themselves ask Jesus for the favor, but in the Gospel of Matthew, it is their mother who kneels before Jesus (a sign of respect in that time and culture) to ask Jesus for the favor of allowing her two sons to sit in the places of honor next to Jesus. In both Gospel versions, Jesus uses the question of who should sit on his right and who should sit on his left as a teachable moment on what it means to be a "servant leader."

Did her sons put her up to it, or is she what we would call a "stage mother" today, trying to get the best roles for her sons? Some people view the mother's question as being presumptuous: "In a culture where a woman's own prestige and status depend primarily on that of her male relatives, such behavior may be presented as understandable, but nevertheless wrong."[1]

As a woman in that time and culture, the mother of James and John took a risk on behalf of her sons and maybe even for herself and her role as their mother in that society. Her question may have been presumptuous and even "wrong"—women then were expected to be largely invisible and silent—but at least she had the courage to ask!

Personal Story

In the era in which I was born and brought up (1940s through 1950s), we were taught that girls and women had very little to say about most things, and religious matters were strictly off-limits. At church where my family attended, we were taught and preached to by males only. Yet, as the elder of my siblings, I was always the ringleader at asking questions of all sorts and presenting concerns for the rest of the crew.

As I grew into adulthood, I was able to ask questions about what was expected of me on the job and any other questions that I needed further explanation for. When it came to questioning the Bible and its context, however, I was always told just to accept what the preacher and teacher taught. I was told, "It is neither good nor proper to question God or God's Word!" I felt as if only those who were teachers or preachers of the Word of God had the right to do the asking.

As I matured and began to attend Bible studies, the expectation of not asking questions, especially those that would cause controversy, became unbearable for me until I came across this Scripture:

> "Ask, and it will be given you; search, and you will find; knock, and the door will be opened for you. For everyone who asks receives, and everyone who searches finds, and for everyone who knocks, the door will be opened. Is there anyone among you who, if your child asks for bread, will give a stone? Or if the child asks for a fish, will give a snake? If you then, who are evil, know how to give good gifts to your children, how much more will your Father in heaven give good things to those who ask him!" (Matthew 7:7-11)

The mother of James and John was brave enough to go to Jesus with her sons to ask that they be granted the honor of sitting on each side of Jesus in his kingdom. She was proud of her sons, and Jesus was gentle in his rebuke, explaining that those seats were reserved for those chosen by God. Many read this Scripture and look down on the mother of James and John for asking such a thing, but oh, to have the confidence in the love of Jesus and to stand before the Savior to make such a brave request!

At Palmer Theological Seminary one of my professors taught us that the only "dumb" question is the one that is not asked. Every question is important and every question we have is a way for us to go to God and trust God to use that question to help us grow. The question is, do *you* trust God with your questions?

In my lifetime I have asked and questioned God about many difficult things, not only about and for my family and friends, but also about decisions that needed to be made. God has always honored my requests by answering, so I have resolved to keep on asking God, who knows all about my future. The Bible reminds me that I did not choose God, but rather God chose me (John 15:16), and that God will answer my questions in the best way possible (Matthew 7:11). I need only to trust God and ask.

Questions

1. What questions would you most like to ask God? What, if anything, is holding you back from taking your questions to God?
2. Is it easier for you to ask questions if it benefits your children or your family than if you need to ask for yourself, and if so, why?
3. What example do you have from your own life when you trusted God enough to ask God your question and God used that question to grow you?

Thought for Your Day

"I never learn anything talking. I only learn things when I ask questions."[2]

Closing Prayer

Dear Lord, help us always to remember that you are our source and are more than sufficient to meet our needs. Let us never be afraid to bring to you all of our questions, our joys, our concerns, our dreams, and our failures, trusting that you will help us live the questions into the answers of our tomorrows. Amen.

About the Writer

Ella M. Parks is a native of Philadelphia. She is a graduate of Phoenix University and graduated from Palmer Theological Seminary of Eastern University with a Master of Theological Studies in Christian counseling. Ella is a teacher of biblical studies at City Wide Interdenominational Christian Training Institute in Philadelphia.

NOTES

1. Carol Meyers, ed., *Women in Scripture: A Dictionary of Names and Unnamed Women in the Hebrew Bible, The Apocryphal/Deuterocanonical Books, and the New Testament.* Grand Rapids (Cambridge, UK: Eerdmans, 2000), 416.

2. Lou Holtz quotes, BrainyQuote.com, www.brainyquote.com/quotes/quotes/l/louholtz384227.html#W8WMd14rO2Gvhi8J.99.

17

Samaritan Woman

Proclaim the Word of Your Witness

TIMOTHY GREENE

> Many Samaritans from that city believed in him
> because of the woman's testimony, "He told me
> everything I have ever done." So when the Samaritans
> came to him, they asked him to stay with them; and he
> stayed there two days. And many more believed
> because of his word. They said to the woman, "It is no
> longer because of what you said that we believe, for
> we have heard for ourselves, and we know that this is
> truly the Savior of the world."
> —JOHN 4:39-42

Hook Question

How do you speak truth?

Biblical Story

JOHN 4:34-42

Jesus said to them, "My food is to do the will of him who sent me and to complete his work. Do you not say, 'Four months more, then comes the harvest'? But I tell you, look around you, and see how the fields are ripe for harvesting. The reaper is already receiving wages and is gathering fruit for eternal life, so that sower and reaper may rejoice together. For here the saying holds true, 'One sows and another reaps.' I sent you to reap that for which you did not labor. Others have labored, and you have entered into their labor."

Many Samaritans from that city believed in him because of the woman's testimony, "He told me everything I have ever done." So when the Samaritans came to him, they asked him to stay with them; and he stayed there two days. And many more believed because of his word. They said to the woman, "It is no longer because of what you said that we believe, for we have heard for ourselves, and we know that this is truly the Savior of the world."

Biblical Exposition

In the Gospel of John, the story of Jesus' encounter with the woman at the well follows several chapters of detailed description concerning just who this Jesus was. The preceding chapters offer a few key connections to the fourth chapter, where our story is found. For example, in John 1:19-34, baptism becomes a focal point. This is the first introduction to water in John's Gospel, which offers significant context for the encounter between the woman at the well and Jesus.

John 2 opens with Jesus attending the wedding at Cana with his mother and his disciples, where water also features prominently, this time in the miracle of turning water into wine (John 2:1-12). By turning water into the choice wine consumed at the wedding, Jesus demonstrated the ability to provide superior nourishment for God's people (v. 10), a theme that surfaces again in chapter 4.

In John 2:13-25 Jesus cleansed the temple and many people believed because of his actions—but the Gospel writer notes that Jesus did not entrust himself to any of them "because he knew all people" (v. 24). This character trait also plays a prominent part in Jesus' encounter with the Samaritan woman at the well.

John 3 records the notable interaction between Jesus and Nicodemus, a Pharisee who sought Jesus out to ask a few questions—and got more than he bargained for. The nighttime encounter between a prominent Jewish leader offers remarkable points of comparison and contrast with Jesus' noontime encounter with a marginalized Samaritan woman. Both conversations feature theological and social aspects and surprising responses from the individuals who engage (or are engaged by) Jesus in dialogue.

One significant connection between Jesus' conversation with Nicodemus and the woman is that Jesus tells the inquisitive Pharisee that the Spirit is like the wind—no one can tell where either will blow. And in the very next chapter, the Spirit "blows" Jesus into a close encounter with a woman (which is unexpected enough) who is also a Samaritan. And as the Gospel writer helpfully notes, "Jews do not share things in common with Samaritans" (4:9).

The Samaritans were a unique people. In many cases they were considered breakaways from the Jewish sect and seen as outcasts. For a Jew to be in the same company as a Samaritan was similar to oil and vinegar mixing. "Samaritans came to be regarded by Jews as neither fully Gentile nor fully Jewish."[1] One of the primary points of contention between the Samaritans and Jews was the appropriate place of worship. Samaritans honored Mount Gerizim as the holy mountain of God, while Jews identified that sacred landmark with Mount Sinai, where the Jerusalem temple stood. Thus, we understand the woman's question to Jesus in John 4:20 as historically and theologically significant.

Even more significant was the power of the woman's witness to her community. While tradition has speculated about the woman's personal history (positing that she may have been promiscuous, a serial monogamist, or a victim of levirate marriage, now living in her father or brother's home), there is no question her testimony about Jesus caused the entire neighborhood to sit up and take notice (John 4:28-30,

39-42). Her witness pushed others to Christ, so much so that a multitude of people went to investigate who this man was: Rabbi, Prophet, Messiah.

Personal Story

For much of my life I was "doing my own thing," keeping up with the latest trends in street life, fashion, music, and most importantly (at that time) money. I alienated some friends and made new ones along the way. I went from choir boy and Sunday school student of the year to becoming a money-hungry flirt who went to church on special occasions and major religious holidays. My mentality at that time was money over everything even if that meant missing holiday meals, sleep, or spending time with family or friends. I was religious, and at the same time, I thought being a money chaser could get me where I needed to be. I was worshipping money while blindly looking for the chance to have a unique encounter with God. It seemed like the longer and longer it took for me to have that mountaintop experience just fed my fuel to be reckless. I used drugs and alcohol because I was looking for the next big thing. One day back in 2005, I was going for a motorcycle ride with some friends when the course of my life changed.

Some friends came to my house and asked if I wanted to go for a bike ride on a Sunday evening—this was a Sunday when I had skipped church and attended "Bedside Baptist" because I was hung over. When my two friends came to the door, I was wearing a tank top and basketball shorts. I was going to ride in my tank top and shorts and sneakers (I had a moment of vanity). As I left the house, something spoke to me to put on my bike jacket, so I ran into the house and put on the jacket. I was ready to ride when that same small voice told me to go back in the house and put jeans and boots on, which I did. As I started the bike and prepared to ride, that same small voice told me to get my helmet. I went from a very relaxed state to a very protected state in a matter of minutes. My friends had no idea what was going on.

Finally, we were able to ride, speeding through the streets of Delaware County, Pennsylvania. About two miles from my house, we were stopped at a red light, and that same voice that told me to put all my clothes on told me to do something that I will never forget. The small voice told me to pray for my life, and I obliged. As people were beeping their horns at me, I did not move until my prayer was finished. If I was going to pray for my life, I was surely going to make sure it was a good prayer!

Several minutes later, at a busy intersection, I flipped my motorcycle, looking up to the sky as I fell off the bike. The two other people I was with could not believe what had just happened, and they came to my aid to make sure I was all right. After rolling about sixty yards, I stood in the middle of the street. Then I fell to my knees and thanked God for saving me. In the midst of my circumstances, I had a unique encounter, and from that moment forth it did not matter where I was, who knew me, or if a person was a complete stranger, I told them how good God is. At that time in my life, I knew God, but I did not really *know* God. It wasn't until I was on my last lifeline that the encounter was meaningful.

Just as the Samaritan woman had a unique encounter with God, I know I did too. She obviously thought that she had the right idea about worship just like I did, but it was not until we both had true encounters that we understood what true worship is.

After the accident, when I would tell people how good God is, most people would turn the other way, but a few bold people were prepared to listen. When I told them about God, I was passionate and enthusiastic. I had met the Lord at a red light, and nothing was going to stop my sharing. We should want our family and friends to investigate how God changes people and not be offended when they say they need to see it for themselves. That is essentially what Jesus is saying in the Scriptures (John 4:34-38). People spend too much time trying to validate you or me when they should be investing in God. For the Samaritan woman, hearing from her family and friends, "It is no longer because of what you said that we believe, for we have heard for ourselves," was liberating. She went from inquirer to messenger, and they sought Jesus because of her word.

When you have a unique encounter with God, God will use you like no one else can. We need to remain focused on the message, focused on the gospel, and everything else will fall into place.

Questions

1. What is your come-to-Jesus story? How does your story compare with that of the woman at the well?
2. What does it mean to be a credible witness? How does your definition line up with the way you have been engaging with others?
3. Who are the individuals in your circle that are bringing truth to light?

Thought for Your Day

It only takes one touch point to change the course of someone's entire life.

Closing Prayer

God, I know that there is none like you, and even in my knowing, sometimes I fall short in recognizing that you are all in all. Help me this day to remember that I am on assignment, an ordained path where I will encounter people, much like Jesus did. Allow me to reach and to touch and to heal and to reconcile in the precious name of Jesus. Amen.

About the Writer

Rev. Timothy Greene is an ordained pastor under the National Baptist Convention and copastor of a church in Delaware County, Pennsylvania. He is a member of the New Hope Baptist Association and a graduate of Palmer Theological Seminary of Eastern University.

NOTES

1. Allen C. Myers, *The Eerdmans Bible Dictionary* (Grand Rapids: Eerdmans, 1987), 907.

18

Joanna

Your Purpose Will Soon Be Revealed; Don't Miss It

KAREN JOHNSON

> "I surrendered my thoughts to God every day when I retreated to that special place in my heart to communicate with Him. That place was like a little slice of heaven, where my heart spoke to His holy spirit, and His spirit spoke to my heart. He assured me that while I lived in His spirit, I'd never be abandoned, never be alone, and never be harmed."
> —IMMACULEE ILIBAGIZA, LEFT TO TELL

Hook Question

Whose somebody are you?

Biblical Story

LUKE 8:1-3

Soon afterwards Jesus went on through cities and villages, proclaiming and bringing the good news of the kingdom of God. The twelve were with him, as well as some women who had been cured of evil spirits and infirmities: Mary called Magdalene, from whom seven demons had gone out, and

Joanna, the wife of Herod's steward Chuza, and Susanna, and many others, who provided for them out of their resources.

Biblical Exposition

Joanna is only mentioned twice in Scripture. We first find her name in Luke 8:3. She is said to be the wife of Chuza, a servant of Herod Antipas. While some Bible translations render Chuza's position as "manager" (MSG) or "household steward" (CEB), indicating that his role was domestic or economic, some scholars have speculated that the centurion in the preceding chapter, Luke 7:1-10 (see parallel in Matthew 8:5-13), might have been Joanna's husband, Chuza.[1] Whatever his specific role in Herod's domain, Joanna's husband held a prestigious position that would have given her status and financial stability. She was able to support a movement that brought her new life (Luke 8:1-3).

Like her more famous companion, Mary Magdalene, Joanna was afflicted with some kind of infirmity, from which Jesus healed her. We don't know anything more than that. Perhaps because of her privileged social position, Joanna had to conceal her affliction from those around her. Perhaps because of her position, she was *able* to conceal it. Joanna's infirmity may not have been physical (Luke 8:3) but a longing to find something she could believe in; social status did not bring joy. It was not until Jesus cured her innermost being that she could experience freedom.

Was Joanna seen only as Chuza's wife and not for the person she was within? Joanna supported Jesus in his ministry along with other unnamed women who received their healing from him. They were the first to arrive at his empty tomb and report back to the disciples (Luke 24:1-12). How magnificent not only to be healed of your physical and mental ills, but also to find your purpose. God used these women in a patriarchal society to announce the most important news the world could ever know. If God had not been revealed through the love of the Son, Jesus Christ, Joanna might never have realized that she was somebody to our creator God.

Personal Story

Did Joanna wonder who she was and what her purpose was in life? I certainly did. I can remember speaking before a group, and one of my oldest acquaintances said, "I didn't know you had it in you." I smiled silently and thought, *It's you, God.*

During the civil rights movement, the poem "I Am—Somebody"[2] bombarded the airwaves and newspapers. These simple words empowered an entire race, those who were oppressed, and anyone who felt out of place or alone in their struggle. I did not identify personally with these words as a youth, because I was not sure what being somebody meant. I was my parent's child and my sibling's sister. I was somebody in the middle—trying to keep up with my older brothers and away from my younger brother and sister. I was basically an obedient child trying to find my place in the family. Accepting Christ at a young age gave me a sense of identity, yet I was still out of place in my own skin. At twenty I became somebody's wife and somebody's mother.

Somewhere in my forties I found my voice. I had something to say and I was somebody. Where did my voice come from? Had I finally grown up? I became aware of self when I began to look back at my life, at all the things I buried deep in my spirit—my hurts and pains, the joys and sorrows. Those very dark memories that I never told to anyone kept me from being somebody. Like Joanna, I was somebody only in relation to my family, but I could not share the somebody within. When God called me to ministry, I knew whose somebody I was. God allowed me to see my childhood experiences as part of life's journey; they were part of my process to become who God needed me to be.

We are God's somebody from birth (Genesis 1:26-27). God's purpose for our lives is planned from the beginning and reveals itself in time. The things we go through to fulfill God's purpose are life's lessons. At times it seems we are nobody's somebody until we go deep inside ourselves and the Holy Spirit reveals God's self to us; then we know for sure whose somebody we are.

Questions

1. Where do you find your strength?
2. What would make your life complete?
3. Immaculee Ilibagiza (see epigraph) surrendered her thoughts to God every day to endure the suffering of her people in Rawanda. What must you surrender to move from bondage to the freedom Jesus' love brings?
4. Whose somebody are you?

Thought for Your Day

"Keep learning from what life brings."[3]

Closing Prayer

God, thank you for your Son, Jesus Christ, in whom we can find our identity. Amen.

About the Writer

Karen Johnson is a licensed minister. She received a diploma in pastoral studies from Eastern University's School of Christian Ministry at Palmer Theological Seminary and is currently working toward a Master of Theological Studies, also at Palmer. Karen serves as associate minister at St. Paul's Baptist Church in West Chester, Pennsylvania.

NOTES

1. Edith Deen, *All of the Women of the Bible* (New York: Harper & Brothers, 1955), 274.

2. "Civil Rights Quotes," Jesse Jackson, www.historylearningsite.co.uk/civil%20rights%20quotes.htm.

3. Anonymous.

19

Tamar

Stumbling into Unsafe Sanctuary

JAMILLA BUTLER STAFFORD

> *Challenging the social norms that condone and therefore perpetuate violence against women is a responsibility for us all.*[1]
> —CLAUDIA GARCIA MORENO

Hook Question

When have you felt hurt or betrayed by someone in the church (or some other place you assumed to be safe sanctuary), and with whom did you share your experience?

Biblical Story

2 SAMUEL 13:10-20

Then Amnon said to Tamar, "Bring the food into the chamber, so that I may eat from your hand." So Tamar took the cakes she had made, and brought them into the chamber to Amnon her brother. But when she brought them near him to eat, he took hold of her, and said to her, "Come, lie with me, my sister." She answered him, "No, my brother, do not force me; for such a thing is not done in Israel; do not do anything so vile! As for me, where could I carry my shame? And as for you, you would be as one of the scoundrels in Israel. Now therefore, I beg you, speak to the king; for he will not withhold me from you." But he would not listen to her; and being stronger than she was, he forced her and lay with her.

Then Amnon was seized with a very great loathing for her; indeed, his loathing was even greater than the lust he had felt for her. Amnon said to her, "Get out!" But she said to him, "No, my brother; for this wrong in sending me away is greater than the other that you did to me." But he would not listen to her. He called the young man who served him and said, "Put this woman out of my presence, and bolt the door after her." (Now she was wearing a long robe with sleeves; for this is how the virgin daughters of the king were clothed in earlier times.) So his servant put her out, and bolted the door after her. But Tamar put ashes on her head, and tore the long robe that she was wearing; she put her hand on her head, and went away, crying aloud as she went.

Her brother Absalom said to her, "Has Amnon your brother been with you? Be quiet for now, my sister; he is your brother; do not take this to heart." So Tamar remained, a desolate woman, in her brother Absalom's house.

Biblical Exposition

Tamar was the daughter of King David. She was delivered into the hands of her rapist by her own father, who had been duped by his scheming son. When she tried to resist, she was hushed, violated, and then discarded by Amnon, her halfbrother. Although her full brother Absalom was enraged at her suffering at the hands of Amnon, he also silenced her.

The account of Tamar's rape seems to be little more than a sidebar in the saga of King David's life. It provided an explanation for the violence that ravaged David's family as Nathan's prophecy materialized (see 2 Samuel 12:10-11). Absalom avenged his sister's rape by killing Amnon, and then he seized his father's throne. As author Renita Weems points out, however, the violence suffered by women in the Bible is often incidental to the main point of a story that is typically about a man.[2] This story was never really about Tamar, nor was Absalom's fratricide really about vengeance for her suffering. It was part of a broader scheme to usurp the throne of his father, David.

In an article published in the *Journal of Psychology and Christianity,* Dr. Mitchell Hicks and colleagues hypothesized that all of the power plays involving Tamar were just the sons' attempts to seek the approval and affection they were not given by their father.[3] Women in ancient Near Eastern culture were considered property of men—first of their fathers (or brothers) and eventually of their husbands. Women's identity and security were tied up in these relationships. Women did not have the same power as men to chart their own courses, determine their own destinies, or fight for the positions they desired.

The trauma to Tamar was furthered when her victimization was not validated. By his silence David seemed to side with Amnon, and Absalom told Tamar not to "take [it] to heart" because Amnon was her brother (2 Samuel 13:20). Then Absalom held on to his rage for two years before activating his plot to kill Amnon. Hicks and his colleagues suggest that Absalom's rage was inflamed by his shame for not protecting his sister and displaced frustration at his father.[4]

It is interesting that nothing more was done to protect Tamar since she was a virgin and the daughter of a king. Virginity was essential to a woman's worth and was seen as "a commodity waiting to be brokered at her father's choosing."[5] Marriage, especially in a royal household, was typically a high-stakes political and economic arrangement. (For David, his first marriage to Saul's daughter Michal positioned him to become the next king of Israel.) So, why didn't David protect Tamar's status for his later use to strengthen or expand his kingdom? Again, Tamar's position seems to be incidental to the story.

With her prospects for marriage gone, Tamar remained in Absalom's house a "desolate woman." The word *desolate* indicates a state of misery or unhappiness, but it can also mean isolated, empty, or barren. It is inferred from the text that because Absalom named his own daughter Tamar that his sister must have died within five to seven years of her rape.[6]

Personal Story

Catcalls. The peering eyes of male passersby. Unwelcomed advances. Being the target of unwanted attention is often considered part of being a woman, which leads men and women alike to believe that it is an acceptable practice. Unfortunately, the church is not always a refuge from such behavior. I have experienced this type of behavior from males in the church more times than I wish to recount. Sometimes it was a one-time occurrence. At others it was an ongoing issue that caused me discomfort. But because I too had colluded with the lie that it was acceptable, I never made an issue of it.

Some years ago, however, I had an experience that left me feeling violated, unprotected, and alone. This did not occur in my church but while serving with a ministry in the area where I lived. I tried to deal with it directly and not involve others because, as the Bible says, "Love covers a multitude of sins" (1 Peter 4:8). I didn't want to damage the reputation of the ministry. I tried every way I could think of to address the unwanted attention and inappropriate behavior. Even though the perpetrator indicated that he understood and apologized, the behavior continued.

I started to feel quite alone in trying to deal with the situation, so I opened up about it. I talked to my family about what had happened. I told my pastor and sought his counsel. I hoped that someone would confront this man on my behalf, but that never happened. Eventually, it got to the point where I no longer felt safe to serve with the ministry and avoided any contact with the ministry and its staff.

Unfortunately, avoidance is not an actual strategy for dealing with problems. After two years, I was forced to come face-to-face with the perpetrator. Unable to run away, I lifted my eyes to heaven and sought God's counsel. I happened to run into the man a few times after that, and he seemed to think our friendship was restored. He called me one day, and rather than ignoring the call, this time I answered. I told him that I intentionally had been avoiding him, that his behavior had continued to have a negative impact on me, and that the friendship could not be restored. I was finally able to communicate clearly and directly. I had been empowered.

Too many women are not empowered in such circumstances. They are more like Tamar, who was not heard when she ran out of Amnon's house crying. Her father did nothing to address Amnon's behavior. Her brother Absalom told her to be quiet and not take it to heart. Tamar's situation was not given the consideration it deserved.

Originally, I felt very much the same way. I was enraged by what I was going through and felt impotent to do anything about it. And there was no one who was likewise enraged enough to come to my aid. Eventually, by seeking God, I was able to find my voice. Tamar, however, was silenced and became invisible. We never hear any more about Tamar in the Bible, and I would imagine that her story is rarely remembered or retold.

Telling Tamar's story can be a corrective. Even though it may be a difficult story to tell and we may not know how best to interpret it, the telling can be life-giving. Though I did not experience violence to the same extent as Tamar (and too many other women in our church pews), I realized as I worked on this chapter that I never named what I experienced accurately. I have always said this person's behavior was "inappropriate" when in actuality it was sexual harassment.

Silencing the victims is a way for perpetrators of violence to maintain power and control. By looking away and not naming sexual harassment or domestic violence as sin, we allow women to continue to suffer. By assuming that victimization is merely a hazard of being female rather than a choice on the part of the males who perpetrate the abuse, we perpetuate the victimization. Remembering Tamar's story (and not allowing it to be forgotten) is one way for the church to be an advocate. It is time for the church to be on the front lines rather than shying away from the reality of domestic violence. The church must stand in solidarity with those who experience sexual harassment, sexual abuse, and domestic violence. Advocating for the victims and allowing their voices to be heard makes the church a safe sanctuary.

Questions

1. When have you cried out for help and had no one come to your aid? How did you react or respond?
2. What policies are in place in your church to address issues of domestic violence, sexual harassment, and sexual abuse? If none, how can the conversation be started to develop them?
3. How else can the church be a place of sanctuary and liberation for those who are suffering?

Thought for Your Day

"To remember what others wish we would forget is powerful stuff."[7]

Closing Prayer

Loving God, help us to tell the difficult stories and give voice to the voiceless. May we actively work toward making your church a safe sanctuary. And when we find ourselves to be the ones crying out with no one to come to our aid, remind us that you are near and we are never alone. Amen.

About the Writer

Jamilla Butler Stafford graduated from Palmer Theological Seminary in 2015 with a Master of Theological Studies. She has a passion for Christian education, missions work, and children. Her call to seminary came after having established a career as a certified school psychologist. She continues to work in this role, serving children with exceptional needs and their families. Jamilla is always amazed at how God uses her passions, training, and various experiences as she continues on this Christian walk, which she calls "the beautiful journey."

NOTES

1. Claudia Garcia Moreno, et. al., *WHO Multi-country Study on Women's Health and Domestic Violence against Women: Initial Results on Prevalence, Health Outcomes and Women's Responses*, report prepared for World Health Organization (Geneva, Switzerland: WHO Library, 2005), vi. http://www.who.int/gender/violence/who_multicountry_study/Introduction-Chapter1-Chapter2.pdf (accessed February 28, 2014).

2. Renita J. Weems, *Just a Sister Away* (San Diego: LuraMedia, 1988), 65.

3. Mitchell W. Hicks, Earl D. Bland, and Lowell W. Hoffman, "Restoring the Voice of Tamar: Three Psychoanalytic Views on Rape in the Bible," *Journal of Psychology and Christianity* 29, no. 2 (2010): 144.

4. Ibid., 145.

5. Ibid., 142.

6. Ibid.

7. Charles S. Hawkins, "Galatians 5:22-23 and 2 Samuel 13—Remembering Tamar," *Review & Expositor* 93, no. 4 (September 1, 1996): 539.

20

Mary Magdalene
What Are You Holding?

JAMES McDOWELL

> *Jesus said to her, "Do not hold on to me."*
> —JOHN 20:17

Hook Question

What is God calling you to do?

Biblical Story

JOHN 20:1-3, 10-18

Early on the first day of the week, while it was still dark, Mary Magdalene came to the tomb and saw that the stone had been removed from the tomb. So she ran and went to Simon Peter and the other disciple, the one whom Jesus loved, and said to them, "They have taken the Lord out of the tomb, and we do not know where they have laid him." Then Peter and the other disciple set out and went toward the tomb. . . . Then the disciples returned to their homes.

But Mary stood weeping outside the tomb. As she wept, she bent over to look into the tomb; and she saw two angels in white, sitting where the body of Jesus had been lying, one at the head and the other at the feet. They said to her, "Woman, why are you weeping?" She said to them, "They have taken away my Lord, and I do not know where they have laid him." When she had said this, she turned around and saw Jesus standing there, but she did not know that it was Jesus. Jesus said to her, "Woman, why are you weeping? Whom are you looking for?" Supposing him to be the gardener, she said to him, "Sir, if you have carried him away, tell me where you have laid him, and I will take him away." Jesus said to her, "Mary!" She turned and said to him in Hebrew, "Rabbouni!" (which means Teacher). Jesus said to her, "Do not hold on to me, because I have not yet ascended to the Father. But go to my brothers and say to them, 'I am ascending to my Father and your Father, to my God and your God.'" Mary Magdalene went and announced to the disciples, "I have seen the Lord"; and she told them that he had said these things to her.

Biblical Exposition

The story of Mary at the gravesite is one of the most popular moments in the gospel story, and with good reason, as Jesus' resurrection is central to the Christian faith. But one person who often gets lost in this story is Mary herself. Who exactly was Mary Magdalene?

Of all biblical characters, it can be said that Mary may be the most commonly misrepresented. She was an individual whom people have portrayed as everything from a prostitute to the mother of Jesus' children. Why are we so confused about who she is? The problem may start in that she was from Magdala (hence being known as "Magdalene"), a place known for poor morals.[1] Then people look to Luke's Gospel, which, unfortunately, makes its first mention of her in chapter 8, after recounting the story of the sinful woman who came before Jesus in chapter 7. When the two points are combined, perhaps the misunderstanding is understandable. Moreover, some interpreters have pointed to the fact that the Gospels of

Mark and Luke testify to her having been possessed by seven demons (Luke 8:2; Mark 16:9), suggesting this as further evidence of her immortality. While she was most certainly cured of the possession, there is no testimony in the Gospels that she had done anything that caused possession. While Scripture offers relatively little detail about her past, what there is seems to indicate she was more of a victim and less of a villain than years of tradition have reshaped her into.

On the other hand, what the Bible does say about Mary is that she was an ardent follower of Jesus and a generous supporter of his ministry. When the women disciples are mentioned, her name is always included, and often she is at the top of the list! We know she witnessed and mourned the death of Christ at the hands of the Romans. We're told in the Gospel of John that she was among the first to see the empty tomb and to tell Jesus' male disciples, who ran to see for themselves. Confused, frustrated, and unsure of what to do next, the men return to their homes, leaving Mary to weep openly and alone.

While Mary Magdalene was probably not the great sinner tradition has portrayed her to be, she *was* fully human and had an incredible amount of love and loyalty toward her Teacher. We can understand her grief. We can relate with her as someone who was suffering from great suffering and loss. Even in the presence of angels, she found herself so emotionally overwhelmed that she failed to appreciate the weight of what was really happening around her.

Then it was the resurrected Jesus who asked her, "Who is it you are looking for?" While Jesus most likely hid his true identity from her at this moment, her response highlighted the depth of her loss but also the expanse of her love for and loyalty to him. The risk involved in reclaiming Jesus' body didn't matter to her at the moment, nor did she seem to consider how she would be able to carry her Lord's body. It was a bold request, and yet it was also thick with irony, as she was talking about recovering Christ's body with the resurrected

Christ. Mary didn't realize that even as she was pleading for some shred of how things were, she was about to receive more than she ever could have dreamed.

In this moment of intense grief, we find ourselves on the brink of one of the most powerful and pivotal moments in the whole of the Bible. With a single word, "Mary," she recognized Jesus for who he was. What happened next is important. Some translations seem to suggest that Mary was stopped short when she tried to embrace the risen Jesus, but most likely that isn't what happened. A better translation of Jesus' words would be "Stop clinging to me." Mary had done exactly what I expect most of us would do in the situation—she had run up to Jesus and was holding on to him for dear life. Her grasp was one of love and desperation, but one that lingered from a fear of this moment.

No, Jesus wasn't keeping her away. Instead, he recognized that like the sorrow that moved her to recover his body at any cost, she was now clinging to him to hold on to this joy. Her unspoken fear was that if she let go, he would be gone once again. So when Jesus spoke, it was with love and the knowledge that neither the sorrow nor the joy could last, not on earth, and most certainly not with work left unfinished.[2]

Releasing Jesus from her grasp, Mary was commissioned as the first person to share the gospel, telling the disciples, "I have seen the Lord."

Personal Story

One day in late February 2013, I sat at my dining room table pondering how life had taken such a downward spin. The prior July life had been perfect. I had been leading a flourishing youth ministry. I was living on my own and was working up the courage to talk with a friend and ministry partner about taking our friendship further. The relationship seemed obvious to many, and a few were actively pushing me to it. The future looked bright, as I was confident that I was on track to become a Methodist pastor in a matter of months. I had been pressured to take on a position at the shore in preparation of the position and the church had been encouraged to begin looking who would take over my youth ministry.

And yet in those few short months, everything had fallen apart. I was being pushed out of my ministry for reasons I didn't fully understand, and in the process I was losing my home. I was paying for bills with student loans and credit cards. To make the situation all the more painful, I had been told that the pastorate was still years away and the woman I loved was in love with another.

My grief was very real, and I desperately tried to cling to any scrap of hope that my life wasn't radically different. I had so quickly gone from having everything, my own home, a promising ministry, a potential relationship—a solid future, and now it was all gone. I wanted to make sense of a situation that seemed senseless. I spent another year trying to look back, trying to cling to my old ministry, my own place, my old life. I kept looking back, wanting nothing more than to go back to the way things were.

At the time of this writing, while I am no longer in that place of grief, the story has not reached the completeness that some may hope for. Some, upon reading this, will expect to read that I reconnected with the object of my affection or that somehow my old youth ministry was restored to me. Others will expect to hear that I'm a Methodist pastor, that I'm married with a family, and that life is better than ever. While I am back in ministry and the Lord has been leading me to begin a church plant, I am currently living with my parents, and I am not in a relationship. While I remain prayerfully optimistic that the Lord has a plan and that things are certainly beginning to play out, I am not quite there yet.

But that doesn't change the fact that I would be entirely ineffective for the Lord if I had refused to leave the gravesite of my old ministry. I, like, Mary could have seen Jesus and yet in my grief mistaken him for the gardener, and thus potentially missed him entirely. Likewise, looking back, I, like Mary, clung on in my joy. My life seemed idyllic, and in my joy, I clung tightly to my blessings, fearful of moving from that place; and in doing so, I was stagnating. In times of joy and comfort, as well as in times of pain and suffering, we, like Mary, can become fixated and overwhelmed. We find ourselves wanting time to stand still or to reverse. But we can allow neither because we have work to do, and we, like Mary, have amazing news to share.

Questions

1. What is God calling you to?
2. What is God calling your group or church to do?
3. What things are you holding on to that need to be released?
4. How do you let go of these things?

Closing Prayer

Lord, lead me as you see fit. Do not let me become stagnant either in my pain or in my comfort. Show me if there is anything that I'm hanging on to that is a hindrance to your plan. Amen.

About the Writer

James McDowell is pastor of Cornerstone Bible Church of Southern New Jersey as well as a student in the Master of Divinity program at Palmer Seminary of Eastern University.

NOTES

1. "Mary Magdalene," All the Women of the Bible, Bible Gateway, www.bible-gateway.com/resources/all-women-bible/Mary-Magdalene.

2. Tremper Longman and David Garland, "John," *The Expositor's Bible Commentary, Luke-Acts* (Grand Rapids: Zondervan, 2007), 647.